Living in Britaly

by Antonia Rocella

Order this book online at www.trafford.com/08-0301
or email orders@trafford.com

Most Trafford titles are also available at major online book retailers.

Note for Librarians: A cataloguing record for this book is available from Library
and Archives Canada at www.collectionscanada.ca/amicus/index-e.html

Printed in Victoria, BC, Canada.

ISBN: 978-1-4251-7292-3 (soft)
ISBN: 978-1-4251-7293-0 (ebook)

*We at Trafford believe that it is the responsibility of us all, as both individuals
and corporations, to make choices that are environmentally and socially sound.
You, in turn, are supporting this responsible conduct each time you purchase a
Trafford book, or make use of our publishing services. To find out how you are
helping, please visit www.trafford.com/responsiblepublishing.html*

*Our mission is to efficiently provide the world's finest, most comprehensive
book publishing service, enabling every author to experience success.
To find out how to publish your book, your way, and have it available
worldwide, visit us online at www.trafford.com/10510*

Trafford Rev. 6/22/2009

www.trafford.com

North America & international
toll-free: 1 888 232 4444 (USA & Canada)
phone: 250 383 6864 ♦ fax: 250 383 6804 ♦ email: info@trafford.com

The United Kingdom & Europe
phone: +44 (0)1865 487 395 ♦ local rate: 0845 230 9601
facsimile: +44 (0)1865 481 507 ♦ email: info.uk@trafford.com

10 9 8 7 6 5 4 3 2

Living In Britaly

Living in Britaly...

.....is a collection of stories and recipes from Britaly ....and just in case anyone ever reads this, I think I'd better explain.........

First of all, I think a formal introduction is in order. My name is Antonia and I'm the Brit part of Britaly. I'm tall, blonde, in my early thirties, with blue eyes and big boobs....... Unfortunately, I'm trapped in the body of an average height, brunette, forty-something with a B cup.......... but, as you can tell, I'm not bitter about it. My husband, Felix, is the Italy part of Britaly. He's easy to describe, quite simply an adorable hedonist. His only imperfection is slightly iffy eyesight, but this actually works to my advantage, 1) because he thinks I'm cute, and 2) he's blissfully unaware of how many pairs of black pants I have in my closet. Together we make up Britaly, our virtual happy place.

This book is mostly about food........and a little bit about life! Actually the two subjects are inseparable if you ask me, because if you get right down to it, life is mostly about food! On the most basic level, we eat to live...... but on a more gastronomically enlightened level, a lot of us live to eat. We eat when we're happy, we eat when we're sad, or in my case, simply because we happen to be awake. Think on.....We eat cake when we celebrate, we eat casseroles when we mourn, we eat pints of Haagen Daas to mend broken hearts and we eat chicken soup to get over the flu. Special event? We've got a dish for it. Easter ham, Thanksgiving turkey, CHRISTMAS PUDDING!!!! Let's face it people, WE EAT! Food is a reward, a joy to be shared, each meal a milestone in our lives. Good food makes life more......well.......everything! Food brings people together, sparks conversation and kindles friendships. It nourishes body, heart and soul........and Fido waiting patiently under the dinner table for errant morsels to fall his way. So you catch my drift? Food is pretty darn important!

But back to Britaly.......Felix invented it because he thought it sounded like a better idea than having a major heart attack at the tender age of 43.........perhaps I should elaborate on that statement.........

Felix is a lawyer, and a good one at that. Unfortunately, along with his chosen career, come certain perks, like *STRESS*, bulging eyeballs, throbbing forehead veins, sky-high blood pressure and strokes. When I first met him, Felix was pretty much charging down Heart Attack Highway at 100 miles an hour, cigarette in one hand, doughnut in the other, feverishly arguing a summary judgment motion in his head. There were virtually no cell phones back then, or he would most certainly have had one clamped between ear and shoulder as well. I think we can safely say he was not stopping to smell any roses and cardiac meltdown was undoubtedly imminent. He is Italian if you remember.

Then one night it all changed. It was about 7:30 p.m., on that dark and stormy evening. I was in the kitchen, slaving over a hot stove, and a cold gin and tonic, when I heard his car careen into our garage, tires screeching like four stepped on cats. The car door slammed, the kitchen door flew open and banged against the washing machine. The smell of burning rubber wafted in from the garage and there he stood, eyes wild, collar open, tie under one ear and briefcase a-dangle. (Picture Jack Nicholson in The Shining and you'll get it.) Anyway, being the prepared sort that I am, I took a deep breath and approached him

1

slowly and quietly, holding out a large, frosty martini. "Hi sweetheart, you're early tonight." I ventured gamely. "Everything okay?" His response (a torrent of blood curdling oaths) killed several completely innocent houseplants in the vicinity and almost singed my eyebrows off. Relieved that my meticulously plucked arches had survived the blast, I arranged them into a suitably fearsome frown and hit him with "the look". Like most women, I am an expert at "the look" and this one took the wind out of his shorts in a big hurry. When the steam coming out of his ears had slowed to mere wisps and that big vein on his forehead had stopped pulsing quite so alarmingly, I gently removed the briefcase and administered the martini.

After dinner and suitably armed with a nice bottle of Chianti, we settled ourselves fireside to ponder Jack Nicholson, life, the universe and everything really. It was obvious we needed to de-stress here……. and buy new houseplants too. Anyway, the obvious answer appeared to be to run away to a sandy beach and drink Margaritas happily ever after. No stress, no Jack Nicholson. Problem solved. We were half way through packing our bikinis and cocktail shakers when we suddenly realized that there might be a tiny flaw in our brilliant plan. Money wasn't a problem, the fact that we didn't have any was. It was true, our retirement fund wasn't even a glimmer in its Daddy's eye. The sofa cushions had yielded only 26 cents and a case-less Rolling Stones CD, which wasn't going to go far……..so our very last hope was……the lottery. Unfortunately, Felix has a troubling history of buying the wrong tickets, and I don't play, so the odds were pretty long on that one too.

Dejectedly, Felix took his shorts off his head and let the bottle of Ban De Soleil slip through his fingers to the floor. It seemed we had no choice but to remain in the rat race, but maybe, just maybe, we could do something different and fun! We retrieved the Sunday classifieds from recycling and devoured them in search of attractive new jobs. Sadly, Professional Beach Bums and Cocktail Testers were not in great demand, and we retreated in a disappointed huddle to the couch. But suddenly, in a blinding flash of genius, it came to him. Felix shot to his feet, and brilliantly channeling James Mason (or maybe it was Winston Churchill) addressed the assembled masses (two snoring dogs, a couple of wildly unimpressed cats and myself)……

"From now on Antonia, this is how it shall be…… You are a Brit and I am Italian, and wherever we are…….we shall be in Britaly. In Britaly, the sun will always be shining and I won't let the turkeys get me down anymore. We will fight them on the beaches……" (Definitely Mr. Churchill there.) "Turkeys? (I'm thinking) we're going to fight turkeys on beaches….and this will help your stress levels how?" But Winston was off again. **"As long as we have each other, a full wine cellar and plenty of snacks, what on earth do we have to worry about? I promise you I will enjoy every day just as much as if we had run away to that beach with the Margaritas. There will be no more wasted days."** He rambled on a lot more, but you've probably got the gist of it by now. Long story short, Felix swore up and down that if he couldn't change the world, then dammit, he would change himself and life really would be a beach. Brilliant!

I quickly got the hang of the whole Britaly idea and dashed off to the kitchen to make a pitcher of Margaritas. Well, as I said, life was now officially a beach and one measly bottle of Chianti doesn't go far you know. For the rest of the evening, we snuggled by the fire and came up with some excellent Britalian rules which, to this day, we strive to live by. Here are just a few of them:

1. Life's a beach…….so feel free to act like you're on vacation.
2. It never rains in Britaly….. sometimes it drizzles liquid sunshine though.

3. Date night is every night.... Casual attire and PJ's okay.
4. Champagne and caviar are not just for special occasions........
5. ....So celebrate something everyday.
6. Bubble baths, fresh flowers and candles are essential for a happy house.
7. Think before opening mouth (unless there is a fork or a glass on the way).
8. Britalian national pastime: Nude sunbathing.
9. No turkeys allowed in Britaly......unless stuffed, basted and roasted.
10. Keep doing what you used to do so you don't have to say "remember when we used to......".
11. Remember to say I love you. You could get run over by a bus tomorrow.
12. No whining!
13. Happy Hours have been formally extended to Happy Weeks.
14. Cherish your friends, and have them over for dinner often.
15. Britalian Motto: Eat Drink Be Merry! Repeat! ......and most importantly.........try very hard to do this every day.......
16. Remember why you fell in love in the first place.

So in essence, Britaly is our name for everything that is good about us and our life.......and we have found that giving it a name makes it much harder to abuse or forget. Of course, I'm sure you've realized that Britaly is also a transparent excuse to eat, drink and make merry to excess, but we like it here, and we're not coming back!

P.S. Over the course of the last decade or so, some very kind, but obviously misguided people who have visited Britaly have told me to record some of its recipes for posterity. I'm not sure if posterity wants them or not, but who knows.......perhaps it will read this someday and feel compelled to make my Lemon Chicken.

The Britalian Kitchen..

The first thing to know about the Britalian Kitchen is that it's exactly like yours. It's not one of those Viking test kitchens, all shiny knobs and 10 million BTU burners (whatever they are). It has a regular four burner stove, a single oven with a thermometer (just in case), burned and otherwise abused wooden spoons, knives that need sharpening, and all the wrong sized baking dishes, yet it still manages to produce some pretty good food on a regular basis. I have been promised a "dream kitchen" when we retire though...... I think I have it written in blood somewhere.

The recipes are favorites that I serve all the time, not some fantasy dishes dreamed up, and tested once, in a kitchen nothing like ours. Most of them are achingly simple and can be attempted by just about anyone. Even people who can kill yeast just by walking down the baking aisle in the supermarket can take a stab at some of these (the ones without yeast anyway). In other words, if my kitchen and I can handle it, you and yours can too.

Next, a few words about the rules and principles of the Britalian kitchen. There's only one of each.

The Rule: Keep It Simple Stupid, or KISS. All those other culinary rules you've heard about can be cheerfully ignored, or broken, in the name of culinary adventure, lack of the right ingredients or, more importantly, better things to do. Facials and pedicures for example. The keep it simple rule is, however, a keeper. I mean, why on earth would anyone want to spend four hours in the kitchen putting chocolate dinner jackets on strawberries, when tuxedo clad fruit can be purchased at Godiva, and you could be getting your pores minimized or your toes tricked out? By all means if you have the time and the inclination, go wild and tackle a tricky soufflé, but only if you're going to enjoy yourself doing it! Otherwise, whip up a quick appetizer, order in a gourmet pizza, pop a silky little Pinot Noir and the evening will still be perfect.

The Principle: Make a valiant attempt to keep recipes heart healthy and non-hip widening. This is because Felix has an Italian heart (a bit of a lemon) and I have a rear end that aspires to be the size of a Volkswagen Beetle. We follow a lot a different "diet" principles, and with this mix and match philosophy, we have so far, kept the old ticker on track, and my rear end from achieving its dream. I try to use whole grain and non fat options as much as possible, but the real things can of course be substituted if your derriere does not have VW tendencies, or if you have already blown the whole day by eating a pint of Haagen Daas Chocolate Peanut Butter ice cream for breakfast and no longer give a damn.

A few things can be made from scratch without violating the KISS rule, but nothing to get all twitched about.....just a tiny bit of domesticity is involved. Trust me, if it put so much as a wrinkle in the fabric of my social calendar, yours truly would not be doing it....... I am a recovering Domestic Goddess you see.

In my callow youth I took homemade from the sublime to well past the ridiculous. I brandied cherries and apricots, I pickled asparagus and beans, I marinated mushrooms and made vats of apple chutney that no one ate. I grew and dried herbs and made flavored oils and vinegars. I preserved lemons for crying out gently. I tell you, if it stood still long enough, I would have it in a Mason jar by the end of the day. Eventually, some dear friends (shocked by the preserved lemons I think) intervened and after several months of intensive spa therapy and shoe shopping, I finally realized that I was not really a Domestic Goddess at all, just a plain, old Goddess. I still have to go to weekly meetings with the girls, but it gets easier every day to buy raspberry vinegar instead of treading the raspberries myself.

Now, weaning oneself off Martha Stewart Living doesn't mean that entertaining with style and aplomb is out of the question. Nor does it mean that I now store shoes in the oven and serve microwaved Hungry Man Dinners. No it does not........I just learned to "cook" a little smarter, and cheat a bit.......okay a lot. With just a few of the following items on hand (most of these keep for ever and so will not go to waste) and maybe a stab at some basic recipes, anyone at all can rustle up a great dinner party, feed unexpected guests, or simply disguise the fact that one has spent all day at Saks and not Safeway:

Pantry:
Crackers
Breadsticks
Croutons
Panko breadcrumbs
Extra virgin olive oil
White truffle oil
Balsamic vinegar (excellent quality and marinating quality)
Sherry vinegar
Red and white wine vinegars
Rice wine vinegar
Tamari sauce
Worcestershire sauce
Tabasco sauce
Anchovies
Marinated and canned artichoke hearts
Canned beans (low salt Garbanzos, Cannellini, Red and Black)
Canned low salt fat free chicken stock
Good tuna packed in oil
Pickled Italian vegetables and asparagus in jars
Cornichons (tiny pickled gherkins)
Canned and pickled quail eggs
Olives (for martinis and nibbling)
Capers
Mango chutney
Various whole wheat pastas
Rice: Brown and wild varieties
Couscous
Polenta
Cracked bulgur wheat

Fridge:
- White wine and Champagne
- Eggbeaters
- Non fat sour cream
- Non fat mayonnaise
- Jar of crushed garlic
- Stone ground mustard
- Crushed ginger
- Seafood cocktail sauce
- Lemons and lemon juice
- Limes and lime juice
- Tomatoes
- Flat leaf parsley
- Fresh basil
- Smoked salmon
- Lox
- Prosciutto
- Miso paste
- Non fat cream cheese
- Non fat Feta cheese
- Parmesan
- Gorgonzola
- Caviar (Domestic is quite good these days. *)

Freezer:
- Roasted red peppers (See Basics)
- Tomato sauce (See Basics)
- Shrimp
- Calamari
- Scallops
- Boneless skinless chicken breasts
- Whole roasting chicken
- Hot Italian sausage (turkey low fat)
- Okra
- Spinach
- Pine nuts
- Walnuts
- Non fat vanilla ice cream

---

* Just because I don't happen to be a Trump or a Hilton, I see no reason to deprive myself of this glorious treat. Domestic caviar is very good these days and very reasonably priced to boot. 1 800 CAVIAR or Tsar Nicolai are good online sources, and if you combine orders with friends you can indulge fairly often. Caviar will keep up to 2 months unopened in the fridge, although I have to admit, this has never been put to the test in my house because we are caviar pigs.

Perfect Pastry
About 1 1/2 lbs of pastry

An easy recipe for perfect pastry......... more difficult to find than Chanel on sale. But here it is. It's a teensy bit difficult to handle at first, but I promise it will become less testy once it has rested in the fridge for an hour or so.

> 2 cups flour
> 1 level tsp baking powder
> 2 pinches salt
> 1 cup butter (very cold) cut into small pea sized pieces
> 2 tbsp non fat sour cream
> 1/3 cup cold non fat milk

Put the flour, baking powder and salt into a bowl and stir around to mix. Cut the butter into the flour with a sharp knife. It helps if you have the butter very very cold; popping it into the freezer for a couple of minutes before you cut it up helps. Next, work the butter into the flour with fingers, or a fork or a pastry blender, whatever method you like. Leave a few lumps of butter; it doesn't all have to be like fine breadcrumbs, which is what they usually tell you. If you leave a few lumps it gives a flakier texture, sort of a sneaky way to flaky pastry. When the butter is worked in to your liking, mix the sour cream into the milk and stir until it's all smooth. Now add the milk mixture slowly to the flour/butter mix, and stir it around with a metal spoon. You may not need all the milk, so keep testing the mix with your fingers to see if the dough will hold together. As soon as you feel you can get it to hold, squeeze it gently into a ball. Don't overwork it whatever you do. The less you manhandle it once the liquid is in, the better, and more tender, the pastry will be. Wrap the ball of dough in cling wrap and put it in the fridge to rest for at least an hour. Then use it at will.

P.S. this will also freeze just perfectly, to be brought out for last minute pies.

San Marzano Tomato Sauce
Makes about 2 cups

This is a quick, fresh tasting sauce, not the kind that has to sit all day long on the back burner.

Canned San Marzano tomatoes, without doubt have the best flavor, and make this sauce far superior to any made with regular old mongrel tomatoes. Felix is very particular about tomato sauce, and I think that if I didn't make it with San Marzanos, he would probably turn into a pumpkin, or something equally dramatic.

Make a big batch of this and freeze it in plastic containers ready for those days when grocery shopping is about as appealing as a round of botox shots.

> 2 tbsp olive oil
> 1 large shallot finely chopped
> 1 tsp crushed garlic
> 1 24 oz can of crushed San Marzanos.
> 1/4 cup of fresh basil or oregano or whatever herb you fancy at the time.
> 1/2 cup dry white wine
> Pinch of sea salt
> Fresh cracked black pepper

To make a small batch, put oil into a large saucepan and turn on heat to medium high. When the pan is hot, put in the shallot and stir about for a minute, then put in the garlic and tomatoes. Now add the chopped herb of choice. I really like basil or marjoram but you can do it with thyme, oregano, sage, tarragon or just plain old parsley.....whatever floats your boat. It's also really good with Herbs de Provence if you're feeling at all French. Now I usually add about half a cup of dry white wine just to give it a little extra oomph. Lastly, the sea salt, a few grindings of fresh black pepper and simmer gently for about 20 minutes, if it gets a little too thick add more wine, or some chicken stock or water.

You can make pasta dishes with this, soups, paella, eggplant Parmesan......whatever you like really. If you want to make a big batch to freeze, just double or triple the quantities. Make sure you label your tomato sauce clearly, as it will look just like stewed rhubarb after a month in the freezer, and rhubarb's not very good on pasta.

Roasted Red Peppers

Store-bought roasted red peppers come in ridiculous little jars and are usually hideously expensive, so roasting and freezing your own is well worth the time, and will save you enough money over the year for at least one pair of shoes. Buy a bunch of red bell peppers or pimientos in high summer when the fruit stands and farms are just about giving them away, roast them and sock them away in the freezer.....Even the supermarkets get as generous as two for a dollar around July and August.

Roasted red peppers are great for revving up just about anything from pork chops to ravioli and they'll also give you a whiff of summertime when you whip a bag out of the freezer in mid winter. Add them to pastas, pizza, soups and sauces, make red pepper aioli, heck eat them out of the freezer bag, they're great.

Once you have secured your red bells at a good price, all you need to do then is wash them off and stick them on cookie sheets or roasting pans. Leave them whole, just as they are (take the little sticky labels off them if they came from the store) and pop them into a 375 degree oven. You don't need to cut them; they don't need oil or anything. How easy is that? And, if you put that Release foil underneath them, you won't even have to wash the pan. This is idiot proof cookery if ever I saw it.

Just roast them, turning them frequently, until they are all soft and the skins are mostly blackened. It's easy to tell when the skins are separated from the flesh and will be easy to peel off. When they get to this stage, get them out of the oven and let them cool on the pans. Once cool, pull them apart with your fingers, peel off the skins and take out the seeds and core. Resist the temptation to wash the seeds off under water as you will lose a lot of flavor that way, just swipe them off with your fingers. Once you have cleaned them, put them in whatever size freezer baggies you want, and freeze a little bit of summer.

Hot Sauce

Makes about 5 cups

I came up with this recipe about a hundred years ago, and have never found anything in a bottle that I like better.................well okay a good Chardonnay, but there are times when you need something a little spicier. Spicy yes, but not one of those "Inferno" types that cause third degree burns. I have a frequent dinner guest who will drink it out of the bottle if you let him, and he still has an esophagus. Anyway, it takes about thirty minutes to make a batch, and I have never met anyone who didn't like it. If you want it a little hotter, you can add a couple of Habanero peppers to the mix, but I wouldn't recommend the straight out of the bottle approach if you do.

> 2 lbs red jalapeno type peppers
> 3 1/2 cups white vinegar
> 3 cups water
> 1/2 cup of sugar
> 6 cloves of garlic chopped roughly
> 2 tbsp dried oregano

First thing you need to do is get the stem, seeds and white membranes out of the peppers. Wear rubber gloves when you do this or you will, without doubt, rub your eyes, or some other tender body part that you value, and you will be in for a world of hurt. Just take a vegetable knife and cut the stem off then scoop out the insides and rinse. Once all the peppers are cleaned put everything into a big soup pot and bring to a boil. Then turn it down to a simmer for about 30 minutes. When the peppers are all soft, pour or ladle into a blender and whiz until completely smooth. You will have to do this in batches of course. Then I just pour into clean jars or bottles and cap them off. You can process them in a water bath if you like, but I have found that as long as you have slightly more vinegar than water in the mix there will be no trouble with spoilage. I'm pretty certain I haven't killed anyone with it yet.

Roasted Garlic

Roasted garlic adds a mellower and rounder taste to things than fresh garlic, but roasting a bulb, when you need it for a recipe, takes too long, so I don't do it, and then I get mad because the dish doesn't taste as good as it should. So.... I decided…...I keep jars of fresh ginger and fresh garlic in the fridge, why not roasted garlic as well.

Heat the oven to 350 degrees. Take 1 large whole head of garlic and cut the top off so you can just see the little cloves inside. Pop it into a small baking dish and drizzle some good olive oil over the top. Pop into the warm oven and bake for half an hour. Cover with some foil and roast for about another 30 minutes, or until the cloves are all nice and soft.

Let the head cool and then pull the cloves apart and squeeze all the garlic out of the individual cloves into a small bowl that has a tightly fitting lid. Pour over lots of olive oil to cover and keep the cloves from spoiling or drying out and pop it in your fridge. It's not a waste of the olive oil either because you can use it for dressings or sautéing whatever you want, just add a little more to keep the cloves covered if you pour some out to use. So now you can dip into your little pot for a roasted clove or some garlic flavored olive oil whenever you want. It's good for flavoring soups and sauces, good for stirring into mashed potatoes or polenta, or great for spreading on toasted French bread with some goat cheese and sun dried tomatoes. I'm not sure, but it probably cleans silver and cures Cholera too......I just haven't tried that yet.

Melanzane

(Marinated Eggplant and Zucchini with Mint and Basil)
Makes one big jar

Felix's Mom makes Melanzane and I have to tell you, it's eggplant heaven. She brought us some as a gift once, and we woofed it down, right out of the jar, in a little under two minutes. Felix of course immediately demanded that I learn to make it myself. This might sound a bit chauvinistic of him but it's really not a problem, because any food Felix loves can always be used as a distraction, and this comes in very handy for a girl who shops like I do. It's like pretending to throw a stick for a dog, and watching said dog run off to where he thinks the stick went..........If I'm slinking in with 9 or 10 shopping bags, I'll greet Felix with "There you are sweetheart, I was thinking of making some MELANZANE in a minute, how does that sound?" and sure enough, his eyes roll back in his head like a great white shark, and off he goes to where he thinks the stick went. The bags and I are in!

My Melanzane has zucchini in it as well as eggplant, because when I first made it, I had about three tons of the damn things in my garden and not enough friends to give it all to. So....it's not really, technically Melanzane, but it is good. Felix loves it in a big juicy, Italian, Foccacia bread sandwich about twice a week..... which is about how often I sneak in with 9 or 10 shopping bags.

> 1 large firm, shiny, lovely eggplant
> 2 large green zucchini
> 1 cup loosely packed fresh mint leaves chopped
> 1 cup loosely packed fresh basil leaves chopped
> 3/4 cup freshly grated Parmesan cheese
> Fresh cracked black pepper
> Bottle of very good extra virgin olive oil
> Bottle of very good balsamic vinegar

First of all slice the eggplant and zucchini into rounds between 1/4" and 1/2" thick. Line a cookie sheet with non stick foil and heat the oven to 375 degrees. Brush both sides of all the zucchini and eggplant rounds with olive oil, place the lightly oiled rounds onto the cookie sheet and season with cracked black pepper. Then bake for 20 to 25 minutes and turn them over once halfway through. They should be nice and soft and lightly browned. Make sure they are well cooked and soft because tough eggplant is as easy to chew as boot leather. You can either do this in batches, or use more than one cookie sheet.

Once the vegetables are cooked through set them aside to cool. Get yourself a wide mouth Mason jar or any glass receptacle with an airtight lid that you can keep in the fridge for a while. (It needs to be leak proof because you have to turn the jar upside down now and again to make sure it all marinates evenly). Okay, now put a thin layer of veggies on the bottom of the jar. Sprinkle with a little of the mint, basil and cheese, then grind some black pepper over it. Drizzle with a little of the olive oil and some of the balsamic vinegar, then add another level of veggies and cheese and repeat. Keep repeating the layers until you have used all the ingredients. Then cover or put the lid on and refrigerate overnight. Turn it upside down and then right side up whenever you remember it. The more the oil and vinegar are distributed and the longer it sits and stews the better it tastes.

You can keep this in the fridge for quite some time, but only if you hide it well.

Salad Croutons

I know.... this might seem a bit Domestic Goddessy when it's so easy to grab a bag of those ready made ones at the store, but PLEASE.......think about your health!! Who knows what they put in those salt ridden little bullets anyway, I bet they'd keep for about 80 years......and that really can't be right can it? Trust me, your body is a temple (even if it does come with saddlebags and love handles) and it doesn't deserve to be desecrated with toxic croutons.

> Leftover bread of any sort you like cut into cubes
> Olive oil
> Garlic powder
> Cracked black pepper
> Dried parsley

Whenever you have left over bread, leave it out on the counter overnight and let it get a little stale. Then cut it into cubes and put into a mixing bowl, drizzle some olive oil over, season with a little garlic powder, black pepper and dried parsley and toss it all together with your hands. Now spread the cubes on a baking sheet in one layer. Pop into a 375 degree oven and bake for about 10 to 12 minutes. Keep checking on them during baking, and move them around a bit if necessary for them to brown evenly. When they are toasted and golden, remove from the oven and let them cool on the tray. When completely cool, transfer to a Ziploc bag and store in a dry place. They will keep for quite some time once toasted, but not if you are careless and leave them lying about. The last batch I made never made it to a salad. I swear the poor things never even cooled down. Eaten right out of the bag they were.

For a bit of variation, sprinkle a little finely grated Parmesan over them after they come out of the oven and let it melt a bit. Really good for a classic Caesar salad.

Pickled Quail Eggs

These are fabulous, because as far as I can gather, tons of people have never had quail eggs before......
and they're usually pretty impressed when offered these. Maybe my friends don't get out as much as
yours, but seeing as how it doesn't involve much time or effort to make these, give 'em a bash anyway.

I use the canned quail eggs which can be found at Asian markets and I stock up whenever I can. I wouldn't
mess with fresh ones, as quail are pretty fast on their feet and notoriously reluctant to lay even if you do
manage to catch one. But seriously, fresh eggs this tiny are hell on wheels to peel and would definitely put
these little bites into the too difficult category.

    2 14 oz cans of cooked quail eggs
    2 cups white vinegar
    1 tsp crushed garlic
    1 tsp hot red pepper flakes
    1 tsp cumin
    10 black peppercorns
    1/2 tsp dried thyme
    1/2 tsp Coleman's Mustard powder
    1 bay leaf

Put everything except the eggs into a small saucepan and bring to a boil. Once the mixture is boiling
you can turn it off, cover it, and let it sit for at least a couple of hours. When the mixture has stewed sufficiently, put your quail eggs into clean glass jars and pour the liquid over the top. You can process these
in a water bath if you like, 10 minutes will do it, but they get eaten so fast in my house, that I don't need
them to have staying power, I just slap the lids on and hide them at the back of the fridge to give them a
fighting chance. If I'm being completely lazy, a Tupperware container with a tight lid has been known to
suffice. They're best left to get nice and pickled for about a week ....but like the Melanzane, you have
to hide them behind something in the fridge to achieve this.

Japanese Cucumber Pickles

Love these, because they're a negative food. In other words, eating them burns more calories than they contain, so essentially (and I wholeheartedly believe this) ......the more you eat the more weight you lose. I'd give up my Manolo Blahnik ankle boots (the ones with the silver chains) for chocolate and bread with similar properties.

> 12 small Japanese cucumbers (try local farmer's market, or use 1 big English one)
> Sea salt
> 2 cups white vinegar
> 2 cups cold water
> 1/4 cup sugar (or honey)
> 1 tsp hot pepper flakes

Wash and cut the ends off the cukes and then slice them into rounds about 1/4 to 1/2 inch thick. Put the rounds into a colander and sprinkle liberally with sea salt. Let this stand over the sink for about an hour, and this will get quite a lot of water out of them. (You can omit the salting bit if you are in a hurry, but I think it helps the texture of the pickles if you have the time and inclination to do it.) While cukes are salting, mix the vinegar, water, sugar and hot pepper flakes in a small saucepan and bring to a boil. Once at a boil turn off heat and let cool a bit.

After they have been salted, rinse the cukes carefully under cold water to remove all of the salt. Pop them into the bowl of your choice and pour over the vinegar mixture. Cover and plonk them in the fridge for as long as you can refrain from eating them. These are great with whole wheat crackers and some smoked salmon for a quick appetizer.

The Britalian Bar...

Felix is legendary among our friends, (for lots of things actually), but most famously for his Cloud Martinis. He actually learned this recipe from his uncle, about 25 years ago, and has been perfecting his technique ever since. He's getting quite good now, and is cautiously optimistic that, with a bit more practice, he might have it down by the time he's 75 or so. Even the local country club has adopted his recipe, and it's now a much requested favorite amongst those in the know. Fame at last, but well deserved; the man can make a cocktail shaker sing and dance.

His repertoire does include other cocktails of course, including a fabulous Cosmopolitan and a mean Lemon Drop. And then there are the other concoctions that we have been afraid to name in case he remembers the recipe and makes them again. These things are dangerous with a capital D, and long naps are usually involved at some point. In fact, whole afternoons have been lost after a couple of Felix specials. These nameless libations usually pop up when he has access to tropical fruits, i.e on a beachy/island sort of vacation. Show the man a mango and a blender and he gets terribly excited. Lack of an exotic locale does not slow him down too much however. He is nothing if not persistent, and is quite capable of whipping up some lethal potion at home, if a vigorous root through the fridge has turned up anything that can potentially be mixed with rum or vodka.

Felix is proud of his bar, and he does have a few rules to keep it running smoothly. One shelf in the freezer must be entirely dedicated to keeping bucket sized Martini glasses frozen and at the ready. Smaller glasses have been made available for ladies since the memorable dinner party at which one female guest spent most of the evening lying under the dining table thanks to one of Felix's "Clouds". She kept us delightfully entertained before she passed out though, a perfect example of why our mothers tell us to always wear clean undies each time we leave the house. Only top quality olives are allowed in Cloud Martinis (onion, jalapeno or blue cheese stuffed are preferred) and Beefeater Gin is the house brand. Bombay Sapphire he categorizes as good, but it's a tad too smooth for his liking, and he deems it best kept for ladies or wimps. He's not so picky about the vodka, but he definitely does not care for Stolichnaya, and has banned it from the bar. He always keeps a suitably elderly single malt scotch on hand to encourage uninhibited after dinner conversation, or canoodling in front of a roaring fire.

Felix has just wandered in with a pitcher of Blood Orange Margaritas to kick off lunch........better set the alarm for 6.......I'd hate to miss cocktail hour.

Cocktails

First things first, simple syrup is equal parts sugar and water simmered until the sugar dissolves and then cooled.

The Cloud Martini:

Take one cocktail shaker and half fill with crushed ice. Pour over this Beefeater Gin and any decent Vodka of your choice. The ratio must be 2 parts gin to 1 part Vodka. Shake vigorously and let stand while you prepare your glass. To do this, take a cocktail stick and spear two suitably stuffed olives. Scoop up a little of the olive juice and rub around the inside of your frozen martini glass. When the glass is suitably "dirtied", deposit the speared olives in it, and then pour the Cloud into the glass.

Il Baccio (The Kiss Martini):

Now these are wicked good. I don't know who invented these originally, but our dear friends Kitty and Beasley make a mean one. There is a little advance preparation necessary in that you have to make cantaloupe infused vodka, which takes about 3 weeks, but it's well worth the wait. All you have to do is take a fifth of vodka and a nice ripe cantaloupe, skin and cut up the latter into bite sized chunks, and then soak them in the former for about three weeks. I do this in a sealed container in the fridge. Easy enough. (Beware of eating too much of the cantaloupe once it is well soaked in Vodka, it tastes great, but it will knock you on your derriere faster than you can say "ouch that's going to leave a mark".)

For one Kiss you need 1 1/2 shots of cantaloupe infused vodka, 3/4 shot of Absolut Kurrant Vodka and a splash (this is the kiss part) of Peach Schnaaps. So double or triple ingredients depending on how many you want to make. Then, pour the ingredients into a cocktail shaker half filled with crushed ice and shake well. Strain into a chilled Martini glass and garnish with a piece of the cantaloupe or an orange twist.

The Cosmopolitan:

I like these (and lemon drops too) because they are served in Martini glasses, which I love for the simple reason that they make a girl look very elegant, even yours truly, but, unlike a Martini, they don't knock yours truly on her butt quite as quickly. Half fill a cocktail shaker with crushed ice. Pour in 1 shot of vodka, 1/2 shot of orange flavored liqueur, 1 shot of cranberry juice and 1/2 shot of lime juice and shake. Strain into frosted Martini glasses and garnish with a little lime peel. I also like a variation of these with pomegranate juice instead of the cranberry.

The Lemon Drop:

Like a lot of the best things in life....sticky, but good. Half fill a cocktail shaker with crushed ice and into this put 1 1/2 shots of Citron Vodka, add 3/4 shot of fresh lemon juice and 1 tsp of sugar. Shake and strain into a frosted Martini glass and garnish with a lemon slice. You can sugar the rim of the glass for even more stickiness if you like.

The Bloody Mary:

Felix says these are the most expensive cocktails ever invented as the first ingredient you need to make them is a 40 foot boat....... because it's on the deck of one of these that Bloody Marys taste best. I notice it doesn't keep him from drinking them at home, or in airports, or anywhere else he can get his hands on one mind you.

Dust the rim of a large chilled tumbler with celery salt then fill with ice, pour over this a shot of Vodka and as much sodium free V8 juice as you wish to dilute it with, add 1 tsp Dimitri's Bloody Mary Mix, (check your local Cash and Carry, this stuff is brilliant) stir well with a celery stick and add 2 jalapeno stuffed olives on a cocktail stick.

The Margarita:

The best thing to come out of Mexico, ever.....no argument about that, but they have to be on the rocks, not one of those blended things. My Mum loves Margaritas; I have a charming photo of her drinking one out of a pint mug. Such a trooper she is. Anyway, the best I have ever had were made with Hornitos Tequila, at a golf course in Huatulco, Mexico. It could have been the fact that the agony of playing golf was over, and anything would have tasted as good, I don't know. I do know that Felix and I always used to leave there in happy mode, despite the pathetic golf scores. This is my attempt at that heavenly mix. Salt the rim of a nice tall tumbler, then pop into the freezer to frost. I just don't like those special Margarita glasses; you can't get enough in them. Get a cocktail shaker or a jug of some description and half fill with crushed ice. Add two shots of Tequila, and just a splash of orange liqueur (Cointreau or Triple Sec or whatever you have) and the juice of a large lime. Now add a quarter cup of simple syrup and shake well. Let it sit for a couple of minutes and then pour into your salted and frosted tumbler. Garnish with an extra wedge of lime. Bliss.......after one of these you won't care if you ever break 100.

We discovered a delicious alternative using blood oranges instead of limes while we were on vacation in St. Martin. Really, really good.

The Daquiri:

Just the thought of one of these conjures up slowly twirling ceiling fans above steamy, tropical bars and mysterious, tanned men in white panama hats. I don't know why that should be because I have never been to a place like that, but anyway. Fill a cocktail shaker half full with crushed ice and add 1 1/2 shots of dark rum, the juice of half a lime and 1 tsp of simple syrup. Shake it all about and strain into a chilled cocktail glass.

The Mojito:

Lovely when you have a crowd over for tapas….. Do love drinks with mint! (A large pot of mint in the garden is essential don't you think.) All you have to do is get a couple of tall glasses, take a small lime and cut into quarters. To each glass add two quarters of the lime and an additional tablespoon of lime juice. Add 1 heaped tsp of sugar. Now throw in 3 or 4 ice cubes and six leaves of mint. Now "muddle" this about a bit, so the mint gets bruised and releases its flavor. Then pour in 2 shots of white rum and a good splash of club soda over the top. Stir well and garnish with fresh mint.

And of course, then there is glorious Champagne..........which, by the way, is not just for special occasions…….I highly recommend it for Sunday mornings.

The Bellini:

Now these are a bit special and very Britalian. You can buy canned white peach puree all over the internet if you want, (even through Amazon.com) or you can buy fresh white peaches and put them through a food mill, but let's not be silly here. The canned puree is pretty expensive, but at least you can have it year round. Prosecco is the preferred sparkly, but whatever champagne you like will do just fine in my humble opinion. All you need is a chilled Champagne flute, put 1 oz of white peach puree in and fill with bubbles.

The Champagne Cocktail:

Serious retro elegance. You need sugar cubes, Angostura bitters, twists of lemon, a little Brandy, and of course Champagne! Splash a couple dashes of the bitters on a sugar cube and drop into a Champagne flute, add 2 teaspoons of Brandy. Now fill with bubbles and garnish with a lemon twist. You can embellish a basic Champagne cocktail in a million different ways, you can use Pear Brandy (my favorite), or Blood Orange juice, Chambord or Crème de Cassis for a Kir Royale.

The Mimosa:

Fill chilled Champagne flute to 3/4 full with decent Champagne, and top off with a smidge of fresh squeezed orange juice. Toss in a baby strawberry if you are feeling fruity, and are willing to forfeit that amount of space in your glass. If not, more Champagne!

The Mint Julep:

Felix doesn't make these very often, and they are a bit on the sweet side for me, but I have to put this in because you absolutely must make them for Kentucky Derby Day, it's the right thing to do. These are traditionally served in silver julep cups, but if you don't have possession of the family heirlooms, don't panic, plain old glass does just fine. First, and most important, select a good Kentucky Bourbon. Put 1 slightly heaped teaspoon of sugar into each glass and pour in 1 tbsp of spring water (Volvic will do if you are lacking a spring in the neighborhood). Add one mint leaf and muddle a bit. Now pour in one shot of that old Kentucky Bourbon. Lastly, fill the glasses to the brim with very finely crushed ice. Very gently stir all the ingredients around to blend. You may want to wipe the outside of the glasses dry as they will perspire a little. Now all you have to do is garnish with lots of mint sprigs and.......it's post time. I think one might have a shot at the triple crown after a couple of these.

Breakfast Brunch & Lunch...

What one needs for breakfast, apart from a Bloody Mary of course, are eggs, which usually come from......

Chickens

One morning, just after the crack of eight 'o' clock, I was in the kitchen getting some caffeine into my system, when I happened to glance out of the window. There on the lawn was a magnificent rooster, all glossy green tail feathers and impressive red comb. In a tight ring around said rooster, were the barn cats, completely goggle eyed. It had feathers, and that usually meant breakfast, but they'd never seen breakfast this big before, and were obviously a bit concerned that if they tried to eat it, "Breakfast" might kick their furry little butts. I was overjoyed, I had always wanted chickens, (children never interested me much) and now here was a prime specimen to start my flock. I grabbed a box of Cornflakes, the closest thing I had to rooster food, and galloped outside to win his heart.

"Foggy" settled in quite nicely, and took to roosting on the fence outside the back door at night. A couple of weeks passed and he showed no intention of leaving. Why would he really, all the scratch a rooster could eat, and he was definitely off the cats' breakfast menu. Confident that he was here to stay, I went out and bought him a wife. She arrived one Friday afternoon, in a large burlap sack. Not a very elegant entrance, but I felt sure he would overlook the ignominy of it all once he saw what a hot chick I'd found for him. Sadly, love at first sight never happened, because he never laid eyes on her. While I was wrestling her out of the sack, Rooster Boy, obviously unaware that I was unloading his intended, pushed off to go digging in the Rhododendrons. His bride-to-be took one look at me; dove straight under the barn….and was never seen again, poor thing.

After this fiasco, I decided to raise him a harem from chicks. So we did the heat lamp/cardboard box thing in the mudroom for several months, and were eventually rewarded with two beautiful Rhode Island Reds, Pansy and Primrose. Foggy was extremely happy with this ménage a trois, (age difference is obviously not an issue in poultry circles) and they set about tearing up my gardens in a most enthusiastic fashion. Apparently, they didn't like the beauty bark on the gardens, but much preferred it scattered all over the driveway.

Anyway, all went along quite nicely, until the large black dog that lived next door, dug his way onto the property one dark night and absconded with the entire harem. All we found in the morning were some telltale feathers and some dark fur…..obviously Pansy did not go without a fight. Foggy was devas-

25

tated….. his tail feathers drooped and he gave up chasing the cats……it seemed he was going to die of a broken heart without his girls.

About a week after the birdnappings and suspected murders, Felix and I were in the garden weeding, and Foggy was mooching about under the rhubarb, when all of a sudden, movement at the top of the paddock caught my eye. …… and there was Primrose, galloping along the fence line. She looked a bit worse for wear…..some rather large bald spots were evident, even from a distance, but she was coming home. Foggy saw her, and took off through the Zinnias at 90 miles an hour to meet her. It was so romantic…. like Wuthering Heights or something. The similarity ended when they actually met up though, because I'm pretty sure Heathcliffe didn't jump on Kathy's back and have his rooster way with her ……well it had been a week I suppose. Sadly, Pansy was never seen again, but we gradually added more hens to the family, Pearl, Poppy, Buffy St. Marie, and Paxo to name a few.

As our charming little flock increased, so did the damage to our gardens. They really had a thing for that beauty bark. One evening, after surveying the results of their latest assault on the Chrysanthemums, we decided that free range was definitely over-rated. After a nice glass of Pinot Noir or three, Felix and I had deluded ourselves into thinking we could build a chicken coop. I'm not very talented with a hammer, and Felix is downright dangerous, but we tried…….and we failed. Prototype I was broken out of faster than you can say Steve McQueen. Prototype II got squashed flat by a snow slide off the barn roof. Prototype III got squashed flat by the collapse of the barn roof that the snow slid off of to squash version II, and the last version was built by professionals.

I learned a lot from all this poultry keeping though…….. 1) Felix knows several more swear words than he lets on, but only uses them when he hits his thumb with a hammer, 2) Chickens love to eat grasshoppers, (really, they do) and…… 3) people who only allow themselves one egg per week don't need to keep chickens.

Huevos Rancheros
For 2

I know a little bit of work seems to be involved here, but if you make this for brunch, thereby killing two meals with one stone, and then demand to be taken out for dinner, it really becomes much more reasonable.

> 1 avocado
> Juice of half a lime
> 1 tbsp finely chopped cilantro
> 1/2 cup crumbled Feta cheese
> 3 tbsp olive oil
> 1 small red onion finely chopped
> 1 tsp crushed garlic
> 1/2 tsp ground cumin seed
> 1 tbsp canned chopped jalapenos
> 4 canned San Marzano tomatoes chopped and 1/2 cup of the juice
> 1/2 cup no salt sweet corn
> 1 cup low sodium black beans drained
> 1/4 cup chicken stock
> 1/2 cup cooked and finely chopped spicy sausage
> 4 flour tortillas (whole wheat healthy ones if you like)
> 4 large eggs
> 2 ozs crumbled queso fresco (or more Feta if you like)

Peel, pit and mash the avocado in a small bowl, add the lime juice and cilantro and mix well. Gently stir in 1/4 cup of Feta cheese. Keep covered and cold.

Heat 1 tbsp of the oil in a medium saucepan until hot. Add the onion, garlic and ground cumin and sauté until the onion starts to get soft. Add the jalapenos, tomatoes, juice, and, corn combine well and put on the back burner to simmer, uncovered, over very low heat. The liquid should be just about gone so the salsa is nice and thick, raise the heat to reduce the liquid if necessary.

In a small saucepan, heat the beans and the chicken stock then smash them with a fork until you have a fairly smooth paste.....don't go mad though, some lumps are good. Stir in the cooked chopped sausage and keep warm.

Preheat oven to 375 degrees. Put the tortillas on a non stick foil lined baking sheet, cover with more foil and pop them into the warm oven for 5 minutes. Heat 2 tbsp of olive oil in a non stick skillet and when it's nice and hot, fry the eggs until barely set. While the eggs are frying, spread the bean mixture thickly over the tortillas sprinkle a little cheese over and then pop them back into the warm oven uncovered. When ready to serve, pull the beaned tortillas out of oven and slide onto plates. Divide hot tomato sauce between plates, top with a fried egg and sprinkle with cilantro and remaining cheeses. Serve with the guacamole on the side and maybe some salsa for extra kick.

Fast Huevos Rancheros
For 2

Aslightly faster version for the Sunday mornings when the spirit is willing but the flesh can't really be bothered and you know you're not getting taken out to dinner.

1/2 sweet onion diced
1 red pepper seeded and diced
1/2 medium zucchini diced
2 tbsp chopped canned jalapenos
4 tbsp olive oil
2 low fat fully cooked sausages
4 San Marzano tomatoes chopped
1 can black beans drained
1/2 cup crumbled Feta
4 flour tortillas (whole wheat healthy ones if you like)

Heat the oven to 400 degrees. Dice/chop the onion, pepper and zucchini. Put 2 tbsps oil in a large non-stick sauté pan and heat to medium high. Once pan is hot, add all veggies and the jalapenos and sauté for 5 minutes, stirring frequently. Slice the sausages into 1/2 inch thick rounds and accidentally eat the end bits. Add the rest to the pan and stir around. Add the chopped tomatoes and stir again. When all is nice and mushy, add 1/4 cup of the Feta, pour everything into a small baking dish and pop into the oven.

Put the drained black beans into a small bowl and sprinkle with 1/4 cup of crumbled Feta cheese. Microwave on high for 3 minutes, stir half way through cooking.

Wrap the tortillas in foil and pop into the oven. Wipe out the sauté pan with some paper towels and add the other 2 tbsp olive oil. Fry the eggs until barely cooked through, they need to be nice and runny. Pull out the tortillas, pop onto plates, top with a couple spoonfuls of the veggie mix, top that with the bean mix and slide the eggs on top of everything. Serve with extra salsa and Tabasco.

Eggs Baked en Cocotte
For 2

This recipe is absolutely to-die-for delicious and perfect for a Sunday morning, after you have read the papers and talked each other out of going to the gym. The truffle paste in this smells so good when they come out of the oven that I have honestly considered dabbing some behind my ears instead of my usual Bond No. 9 Chinatown. If however, by some odd chance it doesn't move you to wear it, I'm sure it will move you to put away the coffee pot and grab some Champagne.

    1 tsp butter
    2 tbsp very finely chopped prosciutto
    4 crimini mushrooms finely chopped
    4 tbsp non fat low sodium chicken stock
    2 slightly rounded tbsp couscous
    4 tbsp non fat sour cream or crème fraiche
    2 tbsp grated Parmesan
    1 tsp white truffle paste or truffle oil
    2 large eggs

In a small pan, gently fry the prosciutto in the little bit of butter until just starting to crisp. Add the crimini mushrooms and sauté until they give up some liquid. Add the stock and couscous to the pan, stir, then cover and take off the heat. Let it stand until the couscous is soft and is at room temperature. Put the sour cream, Parmesan and truffle paste or oil into a small bowl and mix together. Divide the mushroom mixture between two 4" ramekins then top with the cream, cheese, truffle mixture. Lastly, break an egg into each ramekin. Pop the ramekins onto a baking sheet and then bake in the middle of a 400 degree oven until the egg is barely set; about 18 to 20 minutes. The cream will bubble up around the eggs beautifully, and the couscous helps to mop up all the delicious juices. Attack with small spoon or some crusty bread if you prefer. Oh happy Sunday.

Crab Cakes Benedict

For 2 *(with leftover crab cakes)*

I absolutely love eggs benedict, but I just can't eat it because then I have to obsess about what the Hollandaise sauce is going to do to my thighs. So……I've come up with a healthier version…..I suppose it's not technically eggs benedict anymore, as there's no Hollandaise……and there's a crab cake in it for good measure, but it is on an English muffin and there is ham of sorts and a creamy sauce, so as far as I'm concerned Crab Cakes Benedict it is.

Make the crab cakes ahead of time, keep them in the fridge under plastic wrap, and this is a breeze to put together for a romantic brunch. Champagne always goes very well with crab don't you think. Felix thinks it goes with fish and chips too, but that's another story.

For the Crab Cakes
1 medium shallot finely chopped
1 tbsp finely chopped fresh basil
2 tbsp plus 1/4 cup of Eggbeaters (or two small eggs lightly beaten)
1/2 tsp whole grain mustard
2 tbsp mayonnaise
1/4 cup of grated Parmesan cheese
Few dashes of Tabasco
Few dashes of Worcestershire sauce
Cracked black pepper to taste
1/2 lb of crab meat
1/4 cup flour
1 cup of panko breadcrumbs
4 tbsp olive oil

For the Benedict Part
1/3 cup roasted red peppers chopped
1/3 cup non fat sour cream
1/4 cup non fat cream cheese
1 tbsp melted butter
2 whole wheat English muffins
2 large eggs
1/4 cup finely diced prosciutto
1/4 cup finely grated Parmesan
Finely chopped fresh basil for garnish

To make the crab cakes, soak the shallot in boiling water for a couple of minutes, then put into a medium mixing bowl with the basil, the 2 tbsp of the Eggbeaters, (or 1 egg) mustard, mayonnaise, cheese, Tabasco and Worcestershire sauces and the black pepper, and stir it all to mix well. Now squeeze all the liquid you can out of the crab, the drier the better. Dump crab into the mixture in the bowl and use your hands to mix it all together. Now put in 1/2 cup of the panko and mix with hands again. It should be a nice sticky mess. This nice sticky mess now needs to sit in the fridge for at LEAST one hour so the panko absorbs some moisture and the mixture holds together well.

To make the sauce; put the red peppers, sour cream and cream cheese into a food processor and whiz until smooth. Add the melted butter, whiz again briefly and pour into a small saucepan. Get this nice and hot, and then keep warm until you are ready to serve.

When the crab mixture is well rested and ready for its big moment, preheat the oven to 375 degrees. While the oven is heating, put the remaining eggbeaters (or egg) flour and panko crumbs into separate shallow dishes. Now divide the crab mixture into four and form into cakes about the size of English muffins. Once you have formed your four perfect cakes, dip in the flour, then the remaining egg, then into the panko and set them aside on a paper towel or something. Heat the olive oil in a non-stick sauté pan over medium high heat, and make sure the pan is nice and hot before you even think about putting the cakes in. Fry the cakes for 4 to 5 minutes on each side, or until they are nice and golden brown, then pop them into the oven on a foil lined baking sheet for 20 minutes to finish off.

When the crab cakes are almost ready, pop the English muffins alongside them on the baking sheet to toast a little, about 3 minutes. Or you can pop them in a toaster if you prefer. While the muffins are baking or toasting, poach the eggs. Use an egg poacher and save yourself some heartbreak. Trying to get perfect poached eggs out of a pan of water, even with the perfect amount of vinegar, is impossible. As soon as the eggs are barely set up, spread some of the warm pepper sauce on the bottom halves of the muffins. Now place a crab cake on each of the bottom halves, and pop the poached eggs on top. Spoon some more of the red pepper sauce over the top of the eggs then sprinkle with the diced prosciutto and the Parmesan. Almost there now, all you have to do is pop these under the broiler for 30 seconds or so. Finally, lean the toasted top of the muffin rakishly against the side of the stack, sprinkle with chopped basil and serve to riotous applause.

Shrimp Stuffed Baked Avocados
For 2 (for a romantic lunch date)

Had this in a lovely old 16th century pub in England in the summer of 2002, and just loved it. I really wanted a Caesar salad because, as usual, I was trying to thwart my rear end's VW ambitions, but they were a bit short of salads on the menu. I sulked and huffed quite a bit and then grudgingly settled for this. What a spoiled brat…. Just goes to show what trying something new can do for you. I've been making these ever since.

    1/3 cup finely chopped shallot
    1/4 cup non fat cream cheese
    1/4 cup finely grated Parmesan
    1/4 cup non fat mayonnaise
    1/2 tsp hot pepper flakes
    2 large, ripe, but still firm, avocados
    1 3/4 cups salad shrimp squeezed very dry (remove as much water as you can)

Pre-heat the oven to 375 degrees. Soak the shallot in boiling water for 5 to 10 minutes just to take the edge off. In a medium bowl, mix the cream cheese, Parmesan, mayo, and pepper flakes. Drain the shallot, squeeze out the excess moisture and add to the cheese mixture. Cut the avocados in half lengthways and remove the pit. Carefully remove the skin from the avocado and discard. Scoop a tablespoon or so of the flesh out, just to give yourself a bigger hole to stuff the shrimp into, and then mash the excess avocado flesh into the cheese mixture. Add the nicely squeezed shrimp to the cheese mixture and mix together gently. Line a baking dish with non-stick foil and set the avocados in it, cut sides up. You can slice a sliver off the rounded bottoms if you like, just to keep them sitting upright and flat. Spoon the shrimp mixture into the cavities and mound it up nicely. Grind a little fresh black pepper over the tops and pop into the oven for about 35 minutes. Cover with foil for the last 10 minutes if they are getting too browned. Serve with a little salad and a nice grassy Sauvignon Blanc to offset the richness of the avocado.

Lemony Chicken Salad Sandwiches

Makes about 3 cups of chicken salad

Good for field trips, road trips, boat trips and backyard picnics with red checkered tablecloths. Field trip of choice would be a chauffeur driven wine tasting tour, with close friends, on a warm, sunny day. No wine will make it home of course, but what a small price to pay for so much fun.

    1 cup water
    1 cup chicken stock
    1/2 cup lemon juice
    2 boneless skinless chicken breasts
    1 stick of celery finely chopped (pale green from the heart of the bunch)
    1/2 red pepper finely chopped
    1/4 cup non fat mayonnaise
    1/4 cup non fat yogurt
    1 tbsp finely chopped fresh chives
    1 tsp finely chopped fresh tarragon
    1 tsp lemon zest
    Sliced whole grain poppy seed bread (or any nutty bread you fancy)

Heat the water, stock and lemon juice in a medium saucepan until it just simmers, then pop the chicken breasts in. Bring the pan back to a VERY gentle simmer and poach the chicken for 8 minutes. Turn the breasts over and poach for 8 more minutes. Allow the chicken to cool in the poaching liquid. When cool, chop the chicken into very small cubes.

In a large bowl, mix the chicken, celery, pepper, mayonnaise, yogurt, chives, tarragon and lemon zest and season with salt and pepper to taste.

Spread between slices of poppy seed or other whole grain bread and garnish with more fresh chives, oh and some edible flowers like nasturtiums or chive blossoms would be nice too.

The Ultimate Italian
For 1 (Felix)

Only one thing to say about this......guaranteed to turn anyone with a molecule of Italian blood in their veins into a drooling idiot.

  1 small eggplant sliced into 1/4 inch rounds
  1/4 cup olive oil
  1 rustic Italian loaf sliced in half lengthways
  1 small jar artichoke tapenade
  1 small jar black olive tapenade
  1/2 cup roasted red peppers
  1 4 oz log of fresh soft goat cheese
  3 – 4 tbsp good balsamic vinegar
  1/4 lb of good Prosciutto or Serrano ham very thinly sliced
  1 small jar marinated artichoke hearts chopped.
  Small tender leaves of fresh basil and Italian parsley

Pre-heat the oven to 375 degrees. Line a baking sheet with non-stick foil. Brush the slices of eggplant on both sides with the olive oil and place on the baking sheet. Bake in the oven for 10 - 12 minutes, then turn the slices over and bake 10 -12 minutes more. The slices should be browned in places and very soft.

Take your cut loaf and scoop out some of the center on both pieces. If you're using a very flat loaf like a Ciabatta, you don't need to do this scooping. Now spread the artichoke tapenade on the bottom piece and the black olive tapenade on the other piece which will be the lid of your sandwich. Lay the roasted red peppers on the artichoke tapenade then dot half of the goat cheese over the peppers. Throw in some of the fresh herb leaves, and drizzle some of the balsamic over these layers. Layer on the ham and the baked slices of eggplant, dot with the rest of the goat cheese, toss on some more fresh herbs, drizzle with some more balsamic vinegar and finish with a layer of the chopped artichoke hearts. Slap the lid on and give it a good press down. Now wrap the whole thing with plastic wrap as tightly as you can and place the sandwich on a cutting board or large plate. Put another cutting board on the top and stand something very heavy on it, like me, or perhaps a good solid steam iron. Let the sandwich sit with this weight on its mind for at least an hour. Then slice and enjoy.......you might want a bib for this one........catch all that drool you know.

Reubens

For 2

These should be so thick you can hardly get your mouth around them. Eat them only with people you know really well, because it's not pretty.

1 1/2 cups sauerkraut (from the refrigerated section)
1/3 cup non fat sour cream
2 tbsp prepared horseradish
4 slices dark rye bread
2 tbsp whole grain mustard
6 ozs thin sliced pastrami or corned beef
4 ozs thin sliced low fat Swiss cheese
2 tbsp softened butter (or healthy margarine if you like)

Preheat the oven to 375 degrees. Mix together the sauerkraut, sour cream and horseradish in a small bowl. Toast the rye bread slices on one side only. With the toasted side up, spread the mustard over two of the slices, then layer on the pastrami and top with slices of Swiss cheese. Now slather the sauerkraut mixture over the top of the cheese and put the two remaining bread slices on top, toasted side down. Squish together gently and then spread the butter or margarine on the top of the sandwiches. Heat a non stick frying pan over medium high heat and put in the sandwiches, butter side down. While they are in the pan, butter the other side of the sandwiches. Fry for 2 to 3 minutes on each side and then transfer to the oven for 12 to 15 minutes to get nice and hot and melty.

The Bombe

For a small crowd

This is my favorite sort of recipe; looks Cordon Bleu difficult and it isn't. The big ones are really a knockout. I have made them using a huge deep salad bowl for Felix's family's annual golf tournament, and was actually called Martha once or twice. This is one you can make for just a few people. The bowl used here is 8" in diameter and about 4 inches deep. You can use any combination of sliced meats and cheeses that you like. Amounts will depend on the size of bowl you use. Whatever size you decide on, it will knock socks off and leave jaws hanging.

> 1 recipe of pastry (From The Kitchen)
> 1 small eggplant sliced into 1/4 to 1/2 inch rounds
> 1/4 cup olive oil
> 1 tbsp olive oil for sautéing
> 1 cup of finely chopped sweet onion
> 2 cups of frozen chopped spinach (thaw it and then squeeze all the water out of it.)
> 1/2 cup non fat cream cheese at room temperature
> Provolone cheese (sliced)
> Swiss cheese (sliced)
> Pepper jack cheese (sliced)
> Mortadella (sliced)
> Salami (sliced)
> Ham (sliced)
> 1/2 cup basil pesto (store bought will be just fine)
> Roasted red peppers (From The Kitchen)
> 1 large egg lightly beaten

Pre-heat the oven to 375 degrees. Line a baking sheet with non stick foil. Brush the slices of eggplant on both sides with the olive oil and place on the baking sheet. Bake in the oven for 10 – 12 minutes, then turn the slices over and bake 10 - 12 minutes more. The slices should be browned in places and very soft. Take out of the oven and allow to cool completely.

Heat the 1 tbsp of olive oil in a skillet and sauté the onion until it's nice and soft and starting to brown. Put in the spinach and sauté 2 minutes more, then take off the heat and allow to cool completely. Add the cream cheese and stir it all together with a wooden spoon. Set aside.

Take about 1/3 of the pastry dough and set aside. Roll out the remaining 2/3 of the dough to a large circle with the dough 1/4 to 1/2 inch thick. Take your deep pudding bowl and lay the dough circle over it. Push the dough down to line the bowl and let the excess drape over the edges. Put a thin layer of the spinach mixture in the very bottom, then a layer of one of the cheeses, a layer of eggplant slices and then a layer of one of the meats. Spread a layer of pesto over the meat then add a layer of roasted red peppers. Then you repeat these layers, however you please, until you use up all the ingredients.

Next, roll out the remaining small lump of pastry to a circle also 1/4 to 1/2 inch thick. Plop this circle of pastry over the top of the pudding bowl and trim to fit inside the lip of the bowl. Now brush some of the beaten egg around the edge of the pastry circle and then fold the excess from the large circle over the top and seal the edges by pressing gently with your fingers.

Now comes the good bit. Line a large pizza pan with non stick foil (or you can use a baking stone if you have one) and place it, upside down on the top of the pudding bowl, now invert the whole thing and the perfect bombe shaped pie should slip out onto your baking sheet. I decorate it by gently running a sharp vegetable knife very gently over the surface in a swirling pattern. Don't be heavy handed and cut through the pastry, just make tiny grooves. If you have any pastry left, cut out a three or four decorative leaf shapes and arrange over the crest of the bombe. Cut a couple of slits in the top to allow steam to escape then brush with the rest of the beaten egg. Pop it into the oven for about 50 minutes or until the pastry is nice and golden. Cover with some foil if the pastry is getting too dark. (Bigger ones may take a little longer and probably will need to be covered with foil toward the end of cooking to prevent the pastry from over browning.) When perfectly golden, pull out of the oven and cool on a wire rack. Serve at room temperature, sliced into big, beautiful wedges.

Quiche Antonia
Makes one 9" quiche

Who on earth is Lorraine anyway? Here's my version.

For the Crust
    1 recipe perfect pastry dough (from The Kitchen)
    1 lightly beaten egg white

For the Filling
    10 ozs ham chopped (Black Forest would be good)
    2 cups grated sharp Cheddar cheese
    1 cup milk
    1/4 cup non fat sour cream
    6 eggs
    Fresh cracked black pepper
    1/4 cup parsley finely chopped
    1 large tomato sliced

Pre-heat the oven to 375 degrees, then roll out your pastry and lay it into a 10" pie pan with a removable rim, 2" deep. Trim off the overhanging edges, then put a piece of greaseproof paper on the bottom and put in some dried peas or pastry weights to keep the bottom nice and flat. Into the oven and bake for 10 minutes. Remove the peas/weights and paper and pop back into the oven for 5 more minutes. When the crust is nicely golden brush with the lightly beaten egg white and pop back into the oven for 2 minutes, then let cool slightly before you add the filling. Leave the oven on.

Sprinkle the ham and cheese into the pie crust. In a bowl, beat the milk, sour cream, eggs, black pepper and parsley with a whisk until frothy then pour over the ham and cheese. Lay the sliced tomato on top and pop into the oven for about 25 to 30 minutes or until puffed and golden and the center of the pie is just set.

Devonshire Pasties

For 2 large ones, 4 smaller ones, or lots of really little ones.

These were invented by tin miners' wives in the southwest of England hundreds of years ago. There is an ongoing disagreement between the counties of Devon and Cornwall, as to whether they were Devonshire or Cornish wives, but as you have probably gathered from the title of the recipe....... I am from Devon. Anyhow, it's rumored that these clever ladies baked meat, potatoes and various other goodies inside tough packets of dough which they could then throw down the mine shafts when it came around to hubby's lunchtime. The hungry miners, who naturally had nowhere to wash their hands at the bottom of a thirty foot mineshaft, could then hold the dough packets by the crimped edge, and eat the filling without getting their dirty hands all over their food.

These particular pasties are not made with tough dough, so don't try throwing them down any mine shafts, they will not bounce. You can make them any size you like really, big ones for dinner, small ones for snacks. Remember, if you don't have the time or the inclination to make pastry, it's okay, I'm sure you will not be chastised by your miner for using store-bought.

> 1 recipe perfect pastry
> 1 medium potato peeled and cut into 1/4 inch dice
> 1 medium sweet onion peeled and finely chopped
> 1 small rutabaga peeled and cut into 1/4 inch dice
> Salt and pepper for seasoning
> 1/2 lb stewing beef defatted and cut into very small chunks
> 1 tsp butter
> 1 egg beaten and mixed with 1 tsp of water.

Pre-heat the oven to 375 degrees. Mix all the chopped vegetables and meat together in a bowl and season well with salt and pepper. Divide the pastry in half if you are making 2 large pasties and into 4 if making the smaller ones. Roll out each pastry lump into a nice round, about 1/4 inch thick. Place dinner plate face down on the top of each and cut around the edge with a knife. This should give you two perfect rounds to work with. If you want to make the smaller ones, use a salad plate to cut around. Occasionally, I make really little ones for finger food occasions, using a 4" diameter saucer to cut around.

Divide the meat and veggie mix between the pastry rounds, mounding it up in the middle. Put a dot of butter on top of the veggies and meat, and now comes the good part. Brush around the edge of the pastry circle with a little of the egg wash and then bring the sides up over the top of the meat and veggies and crimp the edges together to form a package. Then brush the pasties with the egg wash. Pop the pasties onto a foil line baking sheet and into the hot oven for about an hour for the big ones, about 45 minutes if you're making 4 and for 30 minutes for the 4 inchers. They will come out fragrant, golden and irresistible. Great with HP Steak Sauce believe it or not.

Wild Mushroom Lasagne
One 8x8x2 pan full

This is my version of a fabulous Dean and Deluca recipe. I will admit, it's a little more work than can be expected of a girl on a weeknight, so this is really a special occasion dish and you should be given jewelry, or taken out to dinner every night for a week, if you are kind enough to make this for someone special.

My version is made with fresh pasta instead of dried and I prefer the smoked Provolone to smoked Mozzarella. I have also taken the liberty of lightening up the cream, and adding my favorite accompaniment to mushrooms…..yes, you guessed it, truffle paste. I firmly believe that it absolutely must be made with fresh pasta, as should any lasagne, as it gives it an incredibly light lusciousness that is just not achievable with dried. Having said that, it's your kitchen and if you have dried pasta waiting to be used, or a particularly important waxing appointment with your brow person, then by all means make it with the dried, it will still be delish.

I see you flinching, but really, fresh pasta is not as terrifying as it sounds…..because in order to comply with The Rule of the Britalian Kitchen, you cannot be expected to make it yourself. Any Italian deli worth its gnocchi will have mountains of fresh pasta just dying to be part of your lasagne …..so there's really nothing to be frightened of…..all it takes is a bit of washing. Just like hand washing your delicates really.

> 1 oz dried porcini mushrooms
> 1lb crimini mushrooms
> 8 ozs shitake mushrooms (or any other wild mushrooms you fancy)
> 2 tbsp olive oil
> 2 tbsp butter
> 2 large shallots finely chopped
> 1 tsp finely crushed garlic
> 1/4 cup of very finely chopped fresh sage
> 1/4 cup non fat sour cream
> 1 tbsp white truffle paste (optional)
> 7 4" x 16" fresh pasta sheets
> 1 cup grated smoked Provolone
> 1 cup grated Parmesan

Soak the porcini mushrooms in boiling water for 30 mins. Using a mandoline, very thinly slice the crimini mushrooms. Remove the stems from the shitakes and thinly slice the caps with a knife, (they don't do well on a mandoline). Don't use the shitake stems they're really tough.

Heat 1 tbsp olive oil and 1 tbsp butter in a non-stick sauté pan and when hot, sauté half of the sliced mushrooms until brown and soft. They'll soak up all the oil initially, but then will put out some liquid and things will be fine. When they are nice and brown, remove to a dish and repeat the process with the rest of the oil, butter and the other half of the sliced mushrooms. While the second batch of mushrooms is cooking, add the chopped shallot, garlic and sage. Remove the porcini from the soaking liquid (reserve the liquid) roughly chop and add to the pan along with the previously cooked batch of mushrooms. Add the 1/4 cup of non fat sour cream, truffle paste and some fresh black pepper, stir it all around and set aside.

Heat oven to 375 degrees. Oil an 8 x 8 x 2 baking dish and bring a deep wide pot of lightly salted water to a boil to cook the sheets of pasta. When the water is at a rolling boil, pop in 2 of the sheets for 30 seconds, then remove and rinse under cold tap water. You can treat these sheets like an old dish towel at this point. Literally "wash" them under the running water. This rinsing removes the excess starch and renders them smooth and silky. Once rinsed, lay them flat on clean dish towels to dry off a bit. Repeat with the remaining sheets of pasta until they are all quickly dipped, rinsed and dried. Cover the bottom of your baking dish with a layer of pasta (cut to fit as necessary) then cover with a thin layer of the mushroom mix. Sprinkle a layer of the cheeses over the top of this then add another layer of pasta, mushrooms, cheese etc. Finish with a layer of mushrooms and cheese, then drizzle a couple tbsp of the porcini mushroom soaking liquid over the top, cover with non-stick foil, and pop into the 375 degree oven for 25 minutes then uncover and pop back into the oven for another 10 minutes. Garnish with a few fresh sage leaves if you like. Fungi heaven.

Nibbles Tapas & Small Plates....

I know tapas are not usually associated with Louisiana, but as far as I'm concerned, nibbles definitely are: Felix and I stayed at Chrétien Point in Washington Parish once. I remember the balcony of that magnificent antebellum mansion at sunset. I remember perfect green lawns and ancient pecan trees, resplendent in their garlands of Spanish Moss. I remember an orchestra of cicadas thrumming away in the magnolias. But most importantly, I remember Mary Anne, a charming southern lady, bearing a tray of exquisite little nibbles and two mint juleps (sweating gently in their silver cups). So delicious, I do declare..... I thought I might swoon.

Louisiana

I'll never forget our first trip South. Our six hour flight took ten, all of which were spent sitting next to the poster boy for Camel cigarettes and his four pack per day cough. Lovely. We survived that little preview of hell, only to find that New Orleans had not put out much of a welcome mat for us. In fact, she greeted us with a downpour of biblical proportions, and a night that was darker than a dog's insides. Our rental car, which was supposed to be a sexy little Audi, turned out to be a frumpy little Ford, and we still had a two hour drive, on unknown roads, through alligator infested swamps before we could even think about bed. I was damp, tired and dangerously hungry.....not a good combination for me, as I tend to get.........what's the word........oh yes, bitchy. Felix knows how to distract me though, and he made up a great little game called "Identify the Road Kill". More often than not, neither of us could..........and from this we were able to deduce that we were not in Kansas anymore Toto.

Things did get better. Two days and great dollops of southern hospitality later, I was channeling Scarlett O'Hara. Felix, who frankly couldn't give a damn, was happily eating gumbo for breakfast, lunch and dinner, and fried oysters for snacks in between. We are both adventuresome eaters, and without doubt, Cajun cuisine is an adventure. Really authentic Cajun cuisine on the other hand, is more of a double-dog-dare. I can deal with alligator steak, which by the way does not taste like fishy chicken, it tastes like alligator.... and I relish exotic gumbos, but I will not suck crawfish heads, if you'll pardon the expression, nor will I entertain any dish containing Nutria. Call me a picky eater if you like, but as far as I'm concerned, overgrown, swamp dwelling rats are not menu material. Of course, I suppose if you're an alligator.......or Felix, who will try just about anything that isn't moving and, actually, some things that are!

The whole wonderful thing about rural Louisiana though, besides the southern hospitality and the food, is that it's like stepping back forty years in time. Everything is still legal. Everything! They have drive up Daquiri bars and cockfights for crying out loud. Yes I'm afraid so, and Felix actually made me go to one.

A cockfight, not a Daquiri bar......Obviously, I would have preferred the Daquiri bar. Anyway, I didn't want to go, but Felix insisted that we should experience it.......just once. He's big on experiencing things just once, so, to keep the peace, and because he promised me a pair of Jimmy Choos, I agreed to go along. I will do just about anything for a pair of Jimmy Choos (not the crawfish heads or the Nutria, but most other things). Anyway, I did NOT agree to look at anything, I just agreed to go along.

We arrived in the parking lot, with me clinging to the door of the frumpy Ford.....eyes firmly closed, singing la la la at the top of my voice, and trying desperately to picture my new slingbacks. (This is a denial technique I have perfected for dealing with the numbers on the bathroom scale.) Anyway, Felix peeled me off the Ford and half carried me (still la la la–ing) inside the building. Even over my horrible singing I could hear the bedlam. There was crowing, flapping, dogs barking, kids barking (yes they take their children too) and bookies yelling odds. The place also smelled of sawdust and well......chickens. And let me tell you, chickens, especially in large numbers, really stink.

At this point, I'm feeling a bit queasy, so I ask the girl at the concession stand for a Diet Pepsi, anything to settle the riot going on in my stomach. She fixed me with a suspicious stare and informed me, in the most marvelous southern drawl: **"I'm sorry Sugar, I ain't got no Diet Pepsi......I ain't never had nobody ask me for no Diet Pepsi before,"** (and, most wonderfully of all) **"....and 'sides honey, y'all don't need no Diet Pepsi anyway."** If she'd had two more teeth I swear I would have kissed her.

So there it is, despite the penchant for poultry abuse, I still adore Louisiana because somebody told me 15 years ago that I "didn't need no Diet Pepsi". It's the little things isn't it?

Jalapeño Olives in Jackets

Makes however many olives you have in your jar

Hide them somewhere creative, otherwise these little Cinderellas will not make it to the ball.

    1 jar Mezzetta brand jalapeno stuffed olives
    1/4 cup melted butter
    1 cup Cheddar cheese finely grated
    1 cup flour (plus a bit extra to help with forming)
    1/2 tsp cayenne pepper
    Fresh cracked black pepper
    1/2 cup non fat sour cream

Drain the olives and dry them off as much as possible on paper towels. Melt the butter in the microwave and then cool a bit. In a mixing bowl, combine the cheese, flour, cayenne, black pepper and the sour cream and gently combine into a workable dough. If it's too wet, add a touch more flour, if too dry add a little more sour cream.

Pre-heat the oven to 375 degrees and put a rack in the upper one third. Take a tablespoon sized lump of the dough and mold it around an olive until it is completely covered. Extra flour on the hands helps if the dough is sticking to you and not the olive. Place the jacketed olives on a baking sheet lined with non stick foil and when they all have their coats on bake them for 10 to 15 minutes. You will have to turn them frequently with fingers or tongs so that they brown evenly all over. The jackets will become very malleable and can be remolded to the olives each time you turn them over. When they are golden all over set them to cool on a wire rack.

One can always use Parmesan or any other cheese at hand, Cheddar is not the only option, just make it something with a bit of zip.

Deviled Quail Eggs
Makes however many eggs you have in your can

Another of my favorite recipes because it really impresses people and requires precious little talent. Perfect! Depending on where you live, and who you hang out with, these might get you onto the local A List. If you can look out your window and see farm machinery.......A list. If you can look out your window and see yellow taxis........well anyway, is there a D list?

> 1 16 oz can quail eggs drained.
> 1 tbsp non fat mayonnaise
> Pinch of cayenne pepper
> 1/2 tsp ground cumin
> 1/2 tsp Dijon mustard
> 1 tsp lemon juice
> Finely chopped fresh parsley and grated lemon zest for garnish

Take a small paring knife and take a wafer thin slice off the wider bottom of each egg so they will stand upright. Then, cut off the top of the pointy end about one third of the way down the egg. With a tiny measuring spoon or any suitable weapon really, gently scoop out the yolks into a bowl. You'll get the hang of it once you have wrecked two or three. Just eat the evidence and no one will be any the wiser. Add the mayonnaise, cayenne, mustard and lemon juice and mix until you have a smooth paste.

Now, to get it back into the egg white shells, you can then put the mixture into a piping bag and pipe the mixture back into the eggs, but I make such a hell of a mess with those things, that they are banned from my kitchen. Plus, I would rather gain 10 lbs than wash one of the darn things, so I just scoop it back into the egg white shells with the tiny spoon I used to de yolk them. Arrange your eggs on a pretty platter and scatter the lemon zest and parsley daintily over the top, but don't overdo it.

Pear & Gorgonzola Crostini
Makes a nice big platter for a party

Had something like these at a cocktail party somewhere, many moons ago, and I really don't recall eating anything else that night. I have dallied with other blue cheeses when making these nibbles, but it in the end, it just makes me feel cheap and I come crawling back to my true love.

  1 French baguette
  6 ozs creamy Gorgonzola at room temperature
  2 tbsp Brandy or whatever other hooch you may have to hand (Sherry, Whiskey, Port, they all work)
  1/2 cup pecans
  1 large ripe pear

Pre-heat the oven to 400 degrees. Cover a baking sheet with foil and spread pecans out on it. Roast for about 10 minutes until just browning up, but don't let them burn. Let them cool and then roughly chop them. Save the foiled baking sheet. In a small bowl, mash the Gorgonzola and Brandy together and stir in the chopped pecans.

Cut your baguette into 1/4 inch thick slices, on the angle, and pop them on the same cookie sheet you baked the pecans on. Slide under the broiler until one side is lightly golden. Turn the slices over and lightly toast the second side, but don't overdo it. Cut the pear into quarters and remove the core, then slice the quarters into thin slices and lay them on the toast rounds. Next, spread the cheese mixture over the top and pop under the broiler for 5 minutes or until the cheese gets all melty and bubbly.

You can serve these hot or at room temperature, lord knows they'll be gone in a heartbeat either way.

Eggplant with Honey Mint &Feta

Part of a tapas feast for 4 perhaps?

People might look askance at this until they taste it. But make it anyway; it's good for people to face their fears.

    1 large shiny firm eggplant
    1/3 cup olive oil
    1/4 cup runny honey
    2 tbsp fresh mint finely chopped
    1/4 cup crumbled Feta cheese

Cook the eggplant first using the same method as for Melanzane. i.e. slice into rounds between 1/4" and 1/2" thick. Line a cookie sheet with non stick foil and heat the oven to 375 degrees. Brush both sides of eggplant rounds generously with the olive oil. Then bake for about 10 to 12 minutes on each side. Make sure the eggplant is nice and soft and completely cooked, otherwise it will be tough.

When the eggplant is soft and nicely browned, remove from oven and allow to cool. When it's at room temp, arrange in a single layer on a pretty platter. Now drizzle the honey over it, then crumble the cheese over it and finally scatter the mint and give it a good grinding of fresh cracked black pepper. Now give your guests forks and lead them gently toward the platter making encouraging little noises.

Prosciutto Wrapped Asparagus

Makes however many asparagus spears you have

This excruciatingly simple appetizer is always a big hit. It's not messy to eat, you don't need silverware.....you can wave it at people to emphasize a point......and it's healthy to boot. What more could you ask for?

    1 bundle of thick asparagus spears
    Small head of butter lettuce
    Cherry peppers, olives and/or caperberries for garnish
    1/4 lb very thinly sliced prosciutto
    Jar of whole grain mustard
    Aged balsamic vinegar for drizzling (really old, thick, good quality stuff please)

Wash the asparagus and snap each stalk at the weak point. Put the trimmed asparagus on a large plate, sprinkle a few drops of water over and then cover with plastic wrap. Pop into your microwave on high for 1 minute and test with the point of a sharp knife for doneness. It should be crisp tender, sort of veggie al dente. Once you have the desired result, plunge the stalks into a bowl of iced water to stop the cooking immediately, then drain them and pat dry.

Make a small nest of butter lettuce leaves at each end of a small serving platter and pop a few of your garnishes in each nest. Now lay out a thin piece of prosciutto on a clean work surface and smear it with some of the mustard. Wrap the smeared prosciutto around an asparagus stalk and lay on platter. Repeat until all stalks are wrapped, then drizzle the entire platter with aged balsamic vinegar.

As a variation on this theme, you can use store bought breadsticks instead of asparagus, and wrap the mustardy prosciutto around them. Stand them up in a pretty glass, and pop them in the middle of your table, like a bunch of flowers. These have to be eaten pretty quickly mind, as they will get soggy if left too long. Not usually a problem.

Shrimp with Feta & Scallions
For 4 -6 (as part of a tapas feast)

This is my favorite tapas dish of all time..........no wait.....there's the calamari....

    4 tbsp olive oil
    16 jumbo shrimp peeled and de-veined
    1 clove garlic, minced or crushed
    2 tbsp sherry vinegar
    4 scallions (aka spring onions or green onions) cleaned and chopped
    1/4 cup crumbled Feta cheese
    Fresh cracked black pepper

Put two tablespoons of the oil in a sauté pan and get it nice and hot. Grind some black pepper over the shrimp while the oil is heating. Put the garlic into the hot oil and let it sizzle a little. Then pop the shrimp in and cook for a minute or so on each side. It really only takes two minutes for them to get plump and pink all over. Stir the garlic in and around them to get the flavor all spread about. When they are just cooked through, tip them into a sealable Tupperware type container. In a jar with a tight lid, shake the remaining olive oil and the sherry vinegar together, and then pour it over the still warm shrimp. Crumble the Feta cheese and get the chopped scallions in there as well, then put a lid on it and gently shake it all about. Let this marinate in the fridge for an hour or two, then to serve, pour into your serving dish and garnish with a little fresh ground black pepper. Serve with toothpicks for stabbing, or with some toasted baguette slices for scooping shrimp and soaking in the vinaigrette.

Pan Fried Oysters with Remoulade Sauce

For 2 (as an appetizer)

Make these with ready shucked oysters in jars or pouches to avoid the oyster knife, and thus the inevitable hand injury and associated cussing. If Felix wants fresh shucked, he knows he has to do the shucking, so to speak.

For the Remoulade Sauce

1 cup of non fat mayonnaise
1 tsp spicy mustard
1 tbsp capers drained
1 stick of celery finely chopped
1 shallot finely chopped
1/4 cup chopped Italian parsley
2 tsp paprika
1 tsp red pepper flakes
1 tbsp lemon juice
2 tbsps white wine vinegar
1 clove garlic peeled and crushed
1 good dash Worcestershire sauce
2 canned San Marzano tomatoes drained well and chopped (no juice at all)

For the Oysters

1 dozen shucked oysters (buy jars marked extra small, the yearlings are too tiny).
1/2 cup of flour
1/2 tsp cayenne pepper
Fresh ground black pepper
Salt to taste
1 lightly beaten egg
1 cup panko breadcrumbs
1/3 cup of olive oil for pan frying
Lemon wedges and salad greens for garnish

Place all the ingredients for the remoulade sauce in a food processor blend, transfer to a dish and keep cold.

Dry the shucked oysters on paper towels. In a shallow bowl put the flour, cayenne and black pepper and a sprinkle of salt. In a second shallow bowl put the beaten egg, and in a third shallow bowl put the panko breadcrumbs. Dredge the oysters in flour, then in the beaten egg and then in the breadcrumbs. Put the coated oysters on clean paper towel. When all the oysters are prepared this way, heat the oil until very hot. Put the oysters in and fry on both sides until lightly golden and crisp. Don't crowd the pan with too many, and if you have to do this in two batches, keep the first batch warm in a very low oven. Serve on a nice platter with baby salad greens underneath, and the remoulade sauce alongside. Felix likes them liberally squeezed with lemon juice too. This will make them lose some of their crispness, but as long as you don't mind that, it tastes great.

Marinated Antipasto
For a small crowd

This is another case where you have to try to pretend that carbs are not part of the axis of evil, because it is essential to mop up the juices with good crusty bread. You simply cannot mop this stuff up with a cucumber slice.

1 large red pepper
1 large yellow pepper
1 large orange pepper
5 baby yellow zucchini (I'm talking about 4 inchers here)
5 baby green zucchini (4 inchers too)
2 large bulbs fennel (aka sweet anise)
3 tbsp olive oil
6 hot Italian chicken sausages (use ready cooked ones if you like)
1 pint tiny cherry tomatoes (all colors if you can)
2 8oz pots of Ciliegine (cherry tomato sized balls of fresh Mozzarella, chop up big ones
    if you can't find these little sweeties)
Small handful fresh basil leaves roughly chopped
3 good sprigs fresh oregano (or marjoram) roughly chopped
1 cup olives (your choice, green black, pitted or not)
1/2 cup capers (drained)
Zest and juice of 1 small lemon
2 tbsp sherry vinegar
1/3 cup olive oil
A good grind of black pepper from the mill.

Pre-heat the oven to 400 degrees. Pop the whole peppers onto a foil lined baking sheet and into the oven. Roast, turning frequently, until they are just tender about 15 minutes, then set them aside to cool. Don't let them get too soft, they should still keep their shape and not totally collapse on you. Don't panic if they do though, it'll still taste great. If you're using jarred peppers, just drain and cut into strips.

Slice the zucchini into rounds, trim the fennel bulb of outer tough bits, feathery stalks, and any brown marks, then cut in half lengthways, and then into fairly thin slices. Pop onto a foil lined baking sheet (you may need more than one sheet) and toss with the olive oil. Bake in the same 400 degree oven for about 20 minutes or until tender, but still firm and nicely browned in places. Turn them over or toss them about half way through baking, then set aside to cool.

While peppers and veggies are roasting, cook the sausages fully. You can pan fry them or you can bake them or microwave them, I really don't mind. Microwave makes less mess, but you don't get the nice brown bits on them then. Once cooked, set aside to cool then slice into 1/2 inch thick rounds. Find yourself a large non-reactive bowl or a Tupperware type thingy with a tight fitting lid. Pop your sausages into this and set aside.

When the peppers are cool remove the stems, cut them in half lengthways and remove all the seeds. Peel off all the skin that you can, but don't worry about getting them completely naked, Felix says a little bit of skin tastes just fine to him. Anyway, if you cook the peppers enough to get the skins to completely slip off, they're too floppy and soft for the antipasto in my humble. So once you have them semi-peeled, slice them into about 1/2 inch thick strips and add these and the cooled veggies to the sausage container.

When the sausage and veggies are cool, add the tomatoes, mozzarella balls, herbs, olives and capers and stir it all (gently) about.

Using a fine grater, grate the zest off your lemon. Then cut the lemon in half and squeeze the juice into your salad dressing shaker jar, add the zest, the vinegar, and olive oil and shake well.

Now all you have to do is tip the dressing over the top of the stuff in the bowl. If you have a thing with a lid, put it on firmly and give it all a gentle shake. If you have a bowl, give it all a good stir around with a wooden spoon and then cover with plastic wrap. Stick it in the fridge for at least two days, and shake or stir it often. Serve at room temperature, in a wide shallow bowl, with forks for all and plenty of Italian peasant bread.

Dolmades with Tzatziki
Makes a good big pan-full

Very Greek, but still good to call tapas as far as I'm concerned. Remember, it's your kitchen; you can darn well make the rules. You can serve these hot as a main meal, but I like them room temp, as finger food for parties. They look a lot like short, fat cigars, and in fact, a good friend of ours always complains about how hard they are to light.

For the Dolmades
1 jar grape leaves in brine
1 lb lean ground lamb (use beef if you prefer)
1 medium onion finely chopped
3 large cloves garlic (1 minced and 2 thinly sliced)
1/4 cup fresh mint leaves finely chopped
1/4 cup fresh Italian parsley chopped
2 tbsp dried dill
1/3 cup dried currants
1/3 cup pine nuts
6 ozs tomato puree
1/3 cup Madeira or Sherry
Fresh cracked black pepper
3/4 cup long grain brown rice
2 large lemons
1 cup non fat chicken stock

For the Tzatziki
1 cup non fat plain yogurt
1/2 English cucumber coarsely grated (hothouse or seedless cuke)
1 tbsp fresh mint, finely chopped
1 tbsp fresh dill finely chopped
1 large clove garlic minced or crushed
2 tbsp fresh lemon juice
Fresh cracked black pepper

The most difficult part of this recipe is getting the leaves out of the jar. Thankfully, they are quite tough and can stand a bit of manhandling (or womanhandling in this case). Once you have managed to extricate them from the jar, dump them into a bowl of cold water and rinse off some of the salt. Sort them into two piles, one of puny, ripped and otherwise inferior specimens, and one for the big beautiful intact ones. Take some of the crummy ones and line a baking dish with a single layer. You can use a deep roasting pan or a Pyrex type baking dish, anything about 12" by 16" will do. Next take the beautiful leaves in the second pile and cut the little sticky-out stem off them with a sharp paring knife, one by one and set them aside for stuffing later.

In a large sauté pan, sauté the ground lamb until evenly browned, break up any lumps with your wooden spoon. Pour off any fat that accumulates. Now put in the chopped onion, the 1 minced garlic clove and the herbs. Sauté for about 3 minutes then put in the currants, pine nuts, tomato puree and liquor. Season with black pepper and simmer over low heat for about 20 minutes. Remove from the heat and allow to cool.

While the lamb mixture is simmering for the 20 minutes, cook the rice in plenty of boiling lightly salted water until tender, then drain and allow to cool. When the lamb mixture is ready, stir in the rice, and you have your filling ready to go.

Pre-heat the oven to 375 degrees. Clear yourself a large workspace and start in on stuffing the leaves. Lay a leaf out vein side up with the stem towards you. Take a heaped tablespoon of the lamb mixture and plop it into the center of the leaf. Roll the bottom of the leaf up over the filling, then fold in the sides and roll up the rest of the way until you have the required fat cigar. Stuff all the leaves this way and lay them in the grape leaf lined baking pan. They should be nice and tight together in neat little rows.

Sprinkle the 2 sliced cloves of garlic over the rolls, pour over the chicken stock and the juice of one of the lemons. Slice the other lemon and lay the slices over the top of the dolmades. Cover the dish tightly with foil and bake for 1 hour. Check on the liquid level now and again and don't let it dry out too much, add a little water if necessary. After an hour, most of the liquid should be absorbed, but it should not be completely dry. After the required hour, take the dish out of the oven and allow to cool to room temperature in the baking dish.

While the dolmades are cooling, make the Tzatziki by simply mixing all of the ingredients together, then refrigerate until ready to eat.

To serve, arrange the dolmades on a platter covered with fresh grape leaves if you can find them, or some other greenery if you don't have a vine handy. I leave the baked lemon slices on the top just because they look pretty. Serve a dish of the garlicky Tzatziki on the side for dipping into if you are having them as finger food. If you're using them for a sit down appetizer, put two on a plate and spoon some of the Tzatziki over the top. You can eat these hot too as I said, but always, the Tzatziki is cold. They make a nice light dinner with a little Greek salad.

Spanish Meatballs
Makes 14

They don't know they're Spanish so they don't mind mingling with spaghetti now and again. Besides, if we're going to let the Greek dolmades pass themselves off as Spanish tapas, then surely the Spanish meatballs can pull off Italian pasta if they put their minds to it.

  1/2 lb lean ground beef
  1/2 lb ground veal (or pork)
  1/2 cup fresh breadcrumbs
  1/4 cup finely chopped parsley
  2 tsp dried marjoram
  3 cloves garlic peeled and very finely chopped
  1 large egg beaten
  1/2 cup flour
  Olive oil for frying
  2 large shallots peeled and finely chopped
  3/4 cup dry red wine
  3/4 cup low sodium beef broth
  2 large bay leaves
  2 tbsp tomato puree

Mix the meat, breadcrumbs, herbs, 2 cloves of the garlic, and the egg together in a bowl with your hands and season with salt and pepper. Put the flour in a bowl and then form the meat mixture into golf ball sized balls, roll each in the flour, shake off any excess and line them up on a baking sheet.

Heat a couple tablespoons of the oil in a non-stick sauté pan and sauté the meatballs a few at a time. Make sure they are brown all over. This will take about 8 to 10 minutes per batch. As they are browned, transfer to a plate. You may need to add a little more oil to the skillet for each batch.

In the same skillet heat a little more olive oil and sauté the chopped shallots and the remaining garlic for about 5 minutes. Add the wine, broth, the bay leaves, the tomato puree and stir around, scraping any caramelized bits off the bottom of the pan. Simmer the sauce for about 5 minutes until slightly thickened, then pop the meatballs back in, turn the heat to low, cover the pan and simmer for at least an hour. You can transfer the meatballs and sauce to a covered baking dish and do the hour in a 350 degree oven instead if you prefer. Turn the meatballs occasionally to make sure they are all equally dunked in the sauce. When done, allow them to cool in the sauce. You can serve them hot, or at room temperature, as part of a tapas feast, or as I mentioned earlier, in your spaghetti sauce.

Edamame Dumplings with Dipping Sauce
Makes 28

These are a little bit of a chore to make I suppose, but they are so good, I *sometimes* make an exception to The Rule. Pick a day when you're ahead of the game, fresh nail polish, dogs walked, up to date on magazine and catalog reading etc., then make a double batch and freeze some for next time. You do need one of those two level, bamboo, Chinese steamer basket things for this one. They are cheap, easy to find and a good investment for one's health I think……..You can also wear the lid as a hat if you're hard pressed for a Halloween costume next year.

For the Dipping Sauce
  1/4 cup of low sodium Tamari or soy sauce
  1 tbsp lemon juice
  1 tsp honey
  1/2 tsp hot red pepper flakes

For the Dumplings
  1 1/2 cups (8 ozs) frozen, shelled edamame beans
  2 tsp lemon juice
  2 tsp soy sauce
  1/2 tsp sesame oil
  2 tbsp non fat cream cheese
  1/4 cup chopped green onions (mostly white parts)
  28 gyoza wrappers (or won ton wrappers if you want triangular dumplings)
  4 tablespoons peanut oil (plus a little extra to oil steamer baskets)

Combine all the ingredients for the dipping sauce in a small bowl, making sure the honey completely dissolves, and then let it sit for at least an hour.

Microwave beans with 2 tbsp water, covered, for 5 minutes on high power. They should be nice and soft. Drain and rinse beans in cold water. Put your beans, lemon juice, soy sauce, sesame oil, and cream cheese in a food processor and give it a whirl until you have a fairly smooth paste. You might need to scrape down the sides a couple of times. Turn the paste out into a bowl and mix in the chopped green onions.

Take a gyoza wrapper and place a teaspoon of the bean mixture in the center. Moisten the edges with a little water on a pastry brush and then bring the edges up over the beans and crimp together. As you make them, place the dumplings on sheets of paper towel. Keep the gyoza wrappers you are not working with covered with a damp cloth to keep them from drying out.

When all the dumplings are made, oil the slats of steamer basket with some peanut oil, and bring a pan (roughly the same diameter as your baskets) of water to a simmer. Lay the dumplings in a single layer in both steamer baskets, then, set one on top of the other and place them over the simmering water. Put the lid on, and steam for about 15 - 20 minutes. Switch the position of the steamer baskets half way through steaming, and keep checking the water level in your pan so it doesn't boil dry.

You can serve the dumplings as soon as they are steamed, but I prefer to give them a quick sauté first. This gives them an attractive brown color and they are easier to eat as finger food when sautéed. So, when the dumplings are steamed, let them cool slightly while you heat the peanut oil in a large, non stick sauté pan. When the pan is hot, sauté the dumplings for 1 - 2 minutes on each side, then pop onto paper towels to absorb any excess oil.

You can serve these hot or at room temp. You can serve them on a communal platter as finger food, or you can serve them 2 to 3 to a person on individual plates and drizzle them with the dipping sauce instead. Either way, extra chopped green onions are good for a garnish.

Crab & Shrimp (Crimp) Cakes with Roasted Red Pepper Sauce
Makes 6

My dear friend Nancy dubbed these "Crimp Cakes". Wish I'd thought of that. She's good at names is Nancy......I remember her much beloved cat.......Sophia Maria Penelope Gonzalez Portofino Peecaso. I think she answered to "Kitty" though.

For the Crimp Cakes
2 medium shallots finely chopped
2 tbsp finely chopped fresh basil
1/2 cup of Eggbeaters (or 2 lightly beaten eggs)
1 tsp whole grain mustard
1/4 cup non fat mayonnaise
1/4 cup non fat sour cream
1/4 cup non fat cream cheese
1/3 cup of grated Parmesan cheese
Few dashes of Tabasco
Few dashes of Worcestershire sauce
1 tsp hot red pepper flakes
Cracked black pepper to taste
1/2 lb of crab meat (squeeze all moisture out of it)
1/2 lb of shrimp meat (rinsed, squeezed dry and roughly chopped)
1 3/4 cups of panko breadcrumbs
3/4 cup flour
3 tbsp olive oil

For the Spicy Roasted Pepper Sauce
1/2 cup roasted red peppers coarsely chopped
1/4 cup mayonnaise
1/4 cup non fat sour cream
1/4 cup hot salsa

Put the shallots into a small bowl and cover with boiling water for a couple of minutes, just to take the edge off them. Then drain them and put them into a medium sized mixing bowl with the basil, 1/4 cup of Eggbeaters, (or 1 of the eggs) mustard, mayonnaise, cheese, Tabasco and Worcestershire sauces and the black pepper, and stir it all to mix well. Make sure all the moisture is out of the crab and shrimp, then toss them into the mixture in the bowl and use your hands to mix it all together. Now put in 3/4 cup of the breadcrumbs and mix with your hands again. It should be a nice sticky mess. This nice sticky mess now needs to sit in the fridge for at LEAST one hour so the breadcrumbs absorb some moisture and the mixture holds together well. The mixture can actually sit in the fridge for a few hours with no problem, so you can make it well ahead of time.

When the crab/shrimp mixture is well rested and ready for its big moment, preheat the oven to 400 degrees. While the oven is heating, put the remaining egg and panko crumbs into separate shallow dishes. Now divide crab/shrimp mixture into 6 and form into cakes. You can make them whatever size you like really. Large versions of these make a nice light supper, with a Caesar salad, or small ones are excellent for cocktail party fare.

Once you have formed your perfect size patties, dip them in the flour, then the remaining egg, and then into the panko and set them aside on a paper towel or something. (If you're really short of time, dispense with the eggs and panko and just toss them in a little seasoned flour prior to sautéing. Heat the olive oil in a non-stick sauté pan over medium high heat, and make sure the pan is nice and hot before you even think about putting the cakes in. Fry the cakes for 3-4 minutes on each side, (depending on how big they are) or until they are nice and golden brown, then pop them into the oven for a few minutes to finish off. Large ones will take about 20 minutes in the oven and small ones about 10 minutes.

While the cakes are finishing off in the oven, blend everything for the dipping sauce in a food processor until smooth, pour into a bowl and serve slathered over the hot crimp cakes.

P.S. These are really good with hot pepper jelly as a garnish if you can't be bothered to make the red pepper sauce.

Dips & Spreads...

When it came to the Dips section of this book, I immediately thought about the farm. Firstly because most of the animals we had were definitely dippy, and secondly, because while we lived and toiled like slaves there, we burned so many calories every day we could eat mountains of delectable carbohydrate things, dipped in high calorie stuff, as often as we wanted........ and believe me we did! I think my body was blissfully unaware of the glycemic index back then........ it was probably too tired to notice. Blood sugar?.....what blood sugar?.....zzzzzzzzzz.

I still make dips a lot, but my body is awake and wiser now and has learned to pack on fat if I so much as smell a breadstick. So these days, I keep a wary eye on the carbs and the fat. Oh why do they have to taste so damn good together? Let's face it, unless you're a rabbit, there's no way you're going to prefer cucumber slices as dippers over warm slices of oil and salt slathered pita bread now are you? Maybe with a little hypnosis I could be convinced to give it a try, but.........Nah, it probably wouldn't work on me, and I'd just end up quacking like a duck whenever I heard the word cucumber.

The Farm

When I was young, I actually wanted to be a farmer's wife, live miles from civilization and have enough flour stockpiled in the pantry to make bread for an entire winter. What an idiot! But remember, I was very young and could still eat a loaf of bread a day and not turn into the Pillsbury Dough Girl. Anyway, I got these crazy notions as a result of keeping my ponies on other people's farms for many years. I just loved farms. I was absolutely crushed that my parents showed no interest in quitting their day jobs and taking to the land..... and furthermore, the only livestock we had was a Labrador, with three and a half legs! Now don't misunderstand me, she was a magnificent three and a half legged Labrador, with a bachelor's degree in English, but these farming people had cows and goats and sheep and chickens and and and.......well you get the idea, I was smitten.

There was haymaking, cow milking, sheep shearing and horse riding. There were orphaned lambs in cardboard boxes in the kitchen every spring. There were sheepdogs, baby pigs and the glorious English countryside all around. There was also some pretty potent, homemade, Elderberry wine which might have had something to do with my disturbed state of mind.....but whatever the cause, I loved it all. A handsome young farmer was on the very top of my Christmas list every year....thank heavens I never got one.

Even after I came to the states and met Felix, I still had lingering agricultural yearnings. So......when Felix and I got married, he bought me a pretty farmhouse and LAND. Ten acres of our very own, upon which to grow things, keep noble beasts......... and work ourselves into two exhausted, dirty little monkeys every weekend. I went mad, I really did. I dug raised beds for vegetables, installed overhead sprinklers, planted acres of peonies, iris, lilies, wisteria, daffodils, tulips and roses from England. Felix built me a grape arbor, and we planted more trees than you could shake a stick at. It was beautiful…… and it darn near killed us.

Of course, with all that land, we needed some beasts. We already had faithful Labrador, George, and comedian/pain in the rear cat, Charlie. Next, we were blessed (and I use the term loosely) with two orphaned kittens; one with tail, (Guido), and one without, (Vito Catleone). After some frenzied paddock fencing, Ruben (17 hands of idiot horseflesh), moved home from the livery stables. The move sent the boy into a complete tailspin as there were (horror of horrors) no other horses on the premises……. He spent the first two days burning around the paddock, shrieking his head off like a banshee, and the next two weeks sulking under the curly willow. So……..to appease the poor baby, we acquired Minty, an elegant little chestnut mare, to keep him company. Love at first sight.

Various chickens were gradually added until we had quite the little flock. Then last but not least came Vince, adorable Doberman puppy, who grew from the size of a pot of jam into a small pony, in about 8 weeks. Menagerie complete.

Wonderful memories, but 5 years of agricultural labor is enough to rid any girl of her farming genes. Mowing 3 acres of lawn started to seem less than entertaining, and hauling bales of hay to horses on winter mornings somehow lost its charm. Curiously, I began to long for high heels, weekends in the city…..and fingernails.

Felix decided to start his own law firm, right about the same time that I became allergic to Wellington boots and dirt. This was quite fortuitous actually, because once I'd had it surgically removed from the riding lawnmower, my butt fitted quite nicely into my old business suits. Oh, and having no fingernails really improved my typing speed.

We found lovely homes for the horses and chickens, and still keep in touch with some of the lucky foster parents. Ruben is now a retired 17 hands of idiot horseflesh, and I'm sure all the chickens are long since gone on to free range heaven. The dogs and cats have all passed on too…..except Vito, who is immortal, and has merely gone to live with Grandma.

I miss it all sometimes, moving irrigation pipe, pruning apple trees and weeding till my arms were so tired I couldn't lift a mascara brush. You don't need eyelashes on a farm though, so no biggie. Where was I, oh yes, the mowing, digging, grooming, painting……the dirt tracked into the house, dog/cat/horse hair everywhere and………never mind………somebody hand me my stilettos, I need a manicure.

White Bean Dip with Rosemary Scented Toasts
Makes about 1 1/2 cups

Of course, you can dip cucumber slices into this too if you have been successfully hypnotized.

>About 1/3 cup of very good olive oil
>2 cloves of garlic finely chopped and smashed
>1 tsp fresh very finely chopped rosemary
>1 15 oz can cannellini beans (white kidney beans)
>1 oz Feta cheese
>2 tbsp lemon juice
>Cracked black pepper
>Loaf of ciabatta bread

Put 3 tbsp of the olive oil in a small bowl and add one clove of the garlic and the rosemary. This is for slathering on the bread prior to toasting. Allow the oil to absorb the flavors for at least an hour (or you can use some of the oil from your roasted garlic which should be in your fridge by now).

Drain the beans and reserve the juice. Put the beans, Feta, lemon juice, 1 tbsp of olive oil and about half of the bean juice in a food processor and blend it till smooth. Transfer to a serving bowl. Drizzle the last of the olive oil over the top of the dip (it makes it really luscious) and give it a few grindings of black pepper. Always best at room temperature.

For the toasts: Slice the bread into long thin slices, about 1/4 inch thick if you can, so they will get nice and crisp. Then brush the olive oil, garlic rosemary mixture over both sides of each slice. Put the oiled slices on a baking sheet and toast them under a hot broiler, both sides, until they are crisp and golden.

Arrange the toasted bread around the dip and inhale. (If you don't want to mess with toasting bread, those warmed, oiled and salted pita wedges will also be delicious.)

Crabby Guacamole

Makes about 1 1/2 cups

Ha! Guacamole and not me for a change. (I blame it on the hot flashes).

2 ripe avocados
Juice of 1 small lime
2 tbsp non fat sour cream
Dash of Tabasco
Dash of Worcestershire sauce
1/2 medium sweet onion finely chopped
1 medium tomato finely chopped
1/4 cup finely chopped cilantro
1 tbsp of canned fire roasted chopped jalapenos (you can use fresh if you like)
1/2 cup lump crab meat
2 tbsp crumbled Feta cheese
Fresh cracked black pepper

Cut the avocados in half lengthwise and pry out the pit. Peel the skin off the avocado halves and put them in a bowl with the lime juice. Mash them roughly, but leave a few lumps for texture. Stir in the sour cream, Tabasco and Worcestershire sauce. Now add the chopped onion, tomato, cilantro and jalapenos and gently stir through the mixture. Very gently fold in the crab meat so as not to break it up too much. Transfer to a serving bowl and sprinkle the cheese and black pepper over the top prior to serving. You can scatter a bit more chopped cilantro too if you like. Serve with tortilla chips (or jicama slices) and an extra dollop of sour cream.

Goat Cheese with Artichoke & Olive Tapenades

For 4

This is supremely easy and can be thrown together in a heartbeat, another no skill required winner. (You can use ready made artichoke tapenade if you like).

    1 package frozen artichoke hearts thawed (or 1 can of hearts) thinly julienned
    1 lemon
    2 tbsp good olive oil
    Fresh cracked black pepper
    Greek pita bread (or foccacia bread if you prefer).
    Extra virgin olive oil
    Sea salt
    Small jar of green olive tapenade of your choice
    Small jar of black olive tapenade
    1 log of creamy goat cheese

Toss the artichoke hearts with the juice of the lemon, the olive oil and the black pepper. Brush bread with a little olive oil and sprinkle with sea salt, and then toast in the oven for 5 or 10 minutes and that's pretty much all the cooking this recipe requires of you.

Arrange the log of cheese, and a mound of each of the tapenades on a pretty platter, surround with the toasted pita cut into wedges and off you go. You could go with low fat crackers if you don't want to mess with the pita.

Roasted Elephant Garlic with Sundrieds & Goat Cheese
For 4

Love garlic, especially when it comes supersized like this. Eat this a couple times a week and you will have no cholesterol........and quite probably, no friends either!

    1 head of elephant garlic separated into individual cloves
    3 tbsp olive oil
    2 tsp of fresh oregano (or 1 tsp dried)
    Pinch of sea salt
    1/2 cup sun dried tomatoes (either dry or packed in oil, either will work)
    Fresh cracked black pepper
    Log of goat cheese
    Small loaf of coarse grained Italian type bread
    Greenery for garnish

Pre-heat the oven to 375 degrees. Toss the cloves with the 1 tbsp of the olive oil, 1 tsp of the oregano and the sea salt, then spread them out on a foil lined baking sheet. Bake the cloves for about 20 – 25 minutes, or until the cloves are nice and soft. As soon as they are cool enough to handle, squeeze the garlic out of the skins and set aside. Try to keep the cloves whole if you can.

If you are using dry sundried tomatoes, while the garlic is roasting, soak them in boiling water until totally soft and re-hydrated then roughly chop them. Pour over the remaining 2 tbsp of olive oil and stir in the remaining oregano and black pepper to taste. These should sit for a little while so they absorb all the flavors. If you are using already oil packed tomatoes, you don't need to do a thing to them, except get them out of the jar.

Thinly slice the bread, brush with a little olive oil and pop under the broiler until just golden on both sides.

To serve, garnish a serving plate with some baby greens, pop the goat cheese in the middle, spoon the sundried tomatoes and the roasted garlic around it then arrange the toasty things around the edge of the plate. All you need then are spreaders and hungry people.

Swiss Cheese & Artichoke Dip

Makes about 1 1/2 cups

I'm sure everyone knows this recipe, but just in case......it's ridiculously easy and so good with plain old Wheat Thins. Just right for your favorite low brow crowd.....football fans, teenagers or reality TV watchers, that sort of thing.

    1 cup grated Swiss cheese
    1 cup chopped canned or thawed frozen artichoke hearts
    1 cup non fat mayonnaise

Pre-heat the oven to 375 degrees. Stir it all together and tip into a baking/serving dish. Pop into the oven and bake for 30 minutes until all golden and bubbly. Serve hot with above mentioned Wheat Thins. Remind me now....what time is The Bachelor on?

Baba Ghanoush

Makes about 1 1/2 cups

Strange name, delicious middle-eastern dip. To give it a particularly Britalian twist, instead of roasting your own eggplant, buy a jar of roasted eggplant puree at your local middle eastern store, add the other stuff to it, then go slip into a nice fragrant bubble bath with a good book and a flute of Champagne.

> 2 medium eggplants
> 2 large cloves garlic
> 1 tsp ground cumin
> 1 tbsp fresh lemon juice
> 1 tbsp white wine vinegar
> 1/4 cup extra virgin olive oil (plus extra for drizzling and brushing on eggplants)
> 1/4 cup finely chopped fresh parsley
> Fresh black pepper
> Lemon wedges

Pre-heat oven to 375 degrees. Cut the eggplants in half lengthways, brush with a little olive oil, and then roast in the oven until soft, about 30 minutes. When cool enough to handle, scoop out the flesh into the bowl of a food processor. Roughly chop about half of the eggplant skin and add to the pulp. Add the cumin, lemon juice, vinegar and the 1/4 cup of olive oil to the blender and pulse until smooth. Transfer to a bowl and stir in the parsley. Drizzle with a little more olive oil, season with salt and pepper to taste. Serve with toasted pita wedges and lemon wedges for squeezing over.

Tuna Dip
Makes about 3/4 cup

Now I realize that this sounds like something you'd probably think twice about offering to your cat, but really, it's absolutely delicious. I serve it with whole wheat breadsticks or pita chips, and of course, the ubiquitous cucumber slices, whereupon it actually tastes pretty good.

    1 6 oz can of good tuna packed in olive oil (drained)
    1 large anchovy
    1 tbsp non fat mayonnaise
    2 tbsp non fat sour cream
    1 tbsp lemon juice
    1 tsp balsamic vinegar
    1 tsp Tamari sauce
    Fresh ground black pepper

Put all ingredients into a food processor and blend until very smooth. Ta Da!

Bagna Cauda

For 2

The other hot bath we love.

    1 cup of milk
    10 large cloves garlic, peeled and smashed once with the flat side of the blade of a knife
    3/4 cup olive oil
    1 tsp white truffle oil
    2 cans of anchovy fillets drained and finely chopped
    2 tbsp butter at room temperature
    Chopped fresh parsley for garnish
    Assorted veggies and toasted bread for dipping

You can pretty much use any vegetables you want, cut into bite sized pieces: celery, artichoke bottoms, carrots, zucchini, cauliflower, boiled sliced potatoes, lightly roasted fennel bulb etc. Joy of joy, no cucumber though. The toasted bread is good for holding under the dipped veggies to catch the drips.

In a small saucepan simmer the garlic in the milk until most of the liquid has been absorbed, then puree what is left in a blender along with the olive oil, truffle oil, anchovies and butter until smooth. Return this mixture to the saucepan and simmer very gently for 10 minutes.

Transfer to a small fondue pot, even a dish over a tea light will do, and sprinkle with parsley.

For a more substantial version you can serve boiled shrimp or broiled steak or chicken strips for dipping.

Tabouleh

Makes about 2 cups

This is great because you're actually supposed to serve it with cucumber slices, and of course you can do the toasted pita bread wedges, if your thighs can handle it. Some grocery stores sell a dried Tabouleh mix in the bulk section, and this is fine to use, but you still need to add all the extra fresh ingredients to make it worth eating.

    1 cup cracked bulgur wheat (not too fine)
    1 1/2 cups boiling water
    Zest and juice of 1 large lemon
    1 large clove garlic crushed
    1/4 cup of extra virgin olive oil
    1 tbsp fresh chopped mint
    2 tbsp fresh chopped flat leaf parsley
    2 medium tomatoes diced
    4 inches of an English cucumber diced small
    1/2 medium sweet onion chopped very finely
    Black pepper to taste

Put the bulgur in a large bowl and pour over the boiling water. Add the zest and juice of the lemon and the crushed garlic and stir well. Let this stand, covered with cling wrap until the bulgur is soft. If it's still a little chewy, (this will depend on how finely or coarsely it is cracked) add a little more hot water and give it a few more minutes. It needs to be nice and soft or it's like eating gravel. When the bulgur is suitably "cooked", stir in the remainder of the ingredients and allow the flavors to mingle for at least a couple of hours before serving. It's best at room temperature.

Curried Lentil Dip

Makes about 2 cups

Very good for you lentils are…… carbs that won't play hell with the blood sugar.

    1 cup brown or French green lentils rinsed and drained
    1 1/2 cups water
    1 tbsp curry powder
    1 large clove garlic peeled and smashed to a pulp
    1 6 oz package chopped frozen spinach thawed
    1/3 cup crumbled Feta cheese

Put the lentils, water, curry powder and garlic in a small saucepan and bring to a boil. Turn heat down and simmer until the lentils are tender. Squeeze all the water out of the spinach and stir into the lentils and simmer for another 10 minutes over very gentle heat. Add a little more water if the mix gets too thick. Take off the heat and allow to cool. Stir in half of the cheese and sprinkle the remainder over the top. Serve at room temperature with chips, crackers, pita bread, or guess what….. cucumber.

Smoked Salmon Dip

Makes about 1 cup

The ultimate, easy stand by for unexpected guests. Another Ta Da! recipe to love.

   6 ozs smoked king salmon (preferably wild......or at least mildly annoyed)
   2 tbsp non fat cream cheese
   3 tbsp non fat mayonnaise
   Juice of 1 small lemon (about 3 tbsp)
   Few dashes of Tabasco
   Good dash of Worcestershire sauce
   2 tbsp capers drained
   Fresh cracked black pepper
   Breadsticks, crackers, celery or, yes you guessed it........heck, serve with whatever you feel
      like dipping in it. I just can't say it again.

Put first 6 ingredients into a food processor and whiz until smooth. Stir in the capers, season and refrigerate covered until very cold.

Baked Brie with Mango Chutney
For 4 – 6 (depending on what else you're serving)

You simply can't beat hot cheese for comfort food. This is good served fireside, as a precursor to something rich and French, like that gorgeous hunk Olivier Martinez who played Diane Lane's lover in Unfaithful. If you can't get him, then perhaps a nice Cassoulet might do the trick. Have to be a pretty damn good Cassoulet though wouldn't it?

> 1 6" to 8" wheel of Brie (the kind that comes in a little round wooden box. Beware of "boxes" that are actually cardboard, as they will set your kitchen on fire, and not in a good way!)
> 1 jar of mango chutney (you can actually use any kind of fruity chutney you like, they're all good with nice runny brie)
> Selection of biscuits, or crackers for cheese and crusty bread. (Yay, no cucumber)
> 1 granny smith apple cored and sliced into thin wedges.

Pre-heat the oven to 350 degrees. Unwrap your Brie and slice just the top rind off. Put the Brie back in the bottom part of its wooden box, rind side down obviously. Slather your chutney of choice over the exposed top of the cheese and bake on a baking sheet to catch escaping cheese and juice, just until the cheese is melted, about 30 to 35 minutes. Serve hot, bubbly, and delicious cheese, still in the box, on a nice platter surrounded by the biscuits, crackers, bread and apples.

# Soups...

Soup! Better than Penicillin....... and no needles.

The Flu

I've had the flu. It wasn't pretty. The first signs of deterioration started on a Sunday evening. Nothing drastic, just a bit of a sore throat, and a slight aversion to food and wine. Okay, the last part is pretty drastic, and I should have recognized it as a sign of the horrors to come, but I thought I would be fine with an early night under my belt.

Felix and I had spent the weekend at our little hideaway in Seattle, soaking up some big city culture, and our noses were due back at the grindstone at the crack of dawn on Monday. The grindstone happens to be on the other side of the Cascade mountains, so this meant we would be getting up shortly after midnight. Well okay, 5:30 a.m., but that's uncomfortably close to midnight as far as I'm concerned.

When the alarm went off at this unspeakable hour, I opened one eye (which felt strangely like a hot marble) and glared at Felix's back until he swatted the offending appliance into silence. I cracked open the remaining eye and was rewarded with another hot marble. Hoping I was imagining things, I tried to lift my head off the pillow, only to find it weighed twice as much as when I had put it down there. I gave up, and pondered the possibility of just lying there and pretending it was Sunday again. Pondering hurt too, so I gave that up as well, and just went with the lying there part. Felix gave me a husbandly noogie on his way to the bathroom, and politely requested that I remove my derriere from our matrimonial bed and get the flippin' coffee on. I tried, I really did.

In the end, Felix shoveled me and my pillow into the car, despite my weak protests that he should leave me there to die, and go on with his life. He never listens to me. We eventually arrived home, and the pillow and I were unceremoniously bundled off to the other matrimonial bed, where we both spent the rest of the day praying for a quick and painless death.

Tuesday, the hot marbles were still there, and apparently someone had beaten me with a baseball bat during the night. Oh, and now my teeth hurt too. Needless to say, most of the day was pretty much passed in the same fashion as Monday. At about three 'o' clock I hauled pillow out to the sofa, for a change of scenery, and passed out there until Felix came home at about six. He blew me an air kiss from a safe distance (well I can't blame him, I wouldn't have kissed me either), and then disappeared into the kitchen, while pillow and I returned to our coma on the sofa. When we surfaced again, he'd built a lovely fire and some chicken soup. Give that man a medal somebody. I'm afraid I couldn't really do the soup justice, as my stomach was threatening all kinds of unseemly behavior, but I managed just enough of its wonderful goodness to give me the required energy to drag my fleece clad butt back to bed.

Wednesday dawned a little brighter. Hot marbles had been replaced by eyeballs, albeit each with their own personal headache. The teeth still hurt, and the fellow with the baseball bat had been at it again. I risked a look in the mirror. Bad idea. No wonder this air kiss thing was still going on, in fact it was a wonder Felix wasn't hiding in the hills somewhere. Bloodshot eyes, cracked lips, skin a lovely shade of Exorcist grey, and the stuff on my head defied description. Even my dear Mum would have a hard time loving this. A bath was definitely called for.

It took every last bit of energy, but I got it all washed and dried, only to find it didn't look much better. Still, at least the zombie in the mirror now smelled of orange blossom instead of old pillow.......... which reminded me to jettison my companion of the previous two days, in favor of one from Felix's side of the bed. Well good grief, I was still in no condition to be changing bed linens for heaven's sake. I managed to get halfway dressed too. Fuzzy socks and baggy sweats were the best I could do, but who needs a bra and earrings to watch Good Morning America anyway. After all this upright activity, Felix's pillow and I retreated to the sofa for a nap marathon, interrupted only by a couple of Emeril Live episodes and a slightly larger bowl of that lovely chicken soup.

Thursday. A little better today, but still avoiding the mirror. I was encouraged though, because Felix had risked a kiss on the cheek this morning, so things had to be looking up. I took a short recovery nap after drying the still frightful stuff on my head, and then I paid a visit to the kitchen. I was still at the chicken soup stage, and there was plenty left for me, but Felix had been cooking for himself since Monday and I knew supplies must be getting low. A thorough investigation of the fridge yielded martini olives (naturally) some vintage eggs, a couple sticks of fossilized celery and something frightening in a Tupperware container. Definitely not up to the usual Britalian standards. Okay, whatever the consequences, I was going to have to go out in public. I struggled into some marginally less baggy sweats, managed a pair of earrings and a bra, and hid most of the nightmare hair under a baseball cap. I had to draw the line at makeup though....still way too big a project. Charlie the cat assured me I looked fine to go out into the world, and like an idiot, I believed him. Besides, I'd never see anyone I knew at the grocery store in the middle of a Thursday morning...... would I? Two neighbors, one hairdresser and the cute little fellow from the bank later.......and I was running scared through the vegetable section. Most people just recoiled in horror and made quick getaways, all the faster to spread the news that Antonia had really let herself go, and was probably on drugs to boot. Well, I suppose it could have been worse...at least no one made the sign of the cross or called animal control.

Today is Friday and I'm much, much better. The stuff on my head has mostly turned back into hair, and I have managed the trifecta, earrings, bra AND make up. I'll make Felix a nice dinner tonight.... I think I heard him say something about a sore throat this morning, so perhaps we'd better have chicken soup.

Chilled Summer Soup
For 4-6

These ingredients might sound a bit odd, but it's so good, it's hard not to shovel while eating, or worse, drink it out of the dish. Of course, if there's no one around, who cares! Sup it straight from the blender; and there'll be one less dish to wash.

    3 medium sized, ripe tomatoes roughly chopped
    1/2 large red, orange or yellow pepper seeded and roughly chopped
    1 large clove of garlic crushed with a good pinch of sea salt
    1/2 cup of sourdough bread crumbs (you can use any coarse grained bread you like)
    3 tbsp olive oil
    2 tbsp red wine vinegar
    1 tsp finely chopped fresh marjoram (or oregano) (1/2 tsp if you use dried)
    1/4 cup of good fresh Feta cheese
    1/4 cup finely diced ham (Serrano preferably)
    Nicoise olives for garnish

Put the first 7 ingredients into a blender and pulse until very smooth. Transfer to a bowl season with salt and pepper and refrigerate until cold. Ladle into very small soup bowls (you don't need too much of this soup, just a few mouthfuls really) and sprinkle with Feta and the diced ham. I like the soup bowls on top of salad plates and then I can add a few Nicoise olives and maybe some crispy garlic toasts to the plate for nibbling.

Creamy Cauliflower Soup with Caviar Croutons & Truffle Oil
For 6

I love the smell of truffle oil in the mornings. I prefer the white variety, but black will do almost as well........as I lack my own truffle hunting pig, I tend not to get too picky.

For other variations on this soup, if you have already eaten all the caviar you were trying to keep for two weeks in the fridge, (it's impossible, trust me) you could top the croutons with some black olive tapenade......or you could simply spread the toasted croutons with the goat cheese and garnish (lavishly please) with the truffle oil and some chopped chives.

    2 tbsp olive oil
    1/2 large sweet onion chopped
    1 leek (white part only) cleaned and finely chopped
    1 large head of cauliflower chopped into small pieces (discard the hardest core pieces)
    4 cups low sodium chicken broth
    1 cup of non fat sour cream
    1 cup non fat half and half
    6 thin slices of baguette
    2 ozs goat cheese
    Caviar (your choice)
    White truffle oil
    Fresh cracked pepper

Heat the olive oil in a large pot, sauté the onion and leek until just softened, but not browned and then add the cauliflower bits. Stir about for a minute or two and then add the broth. Season with salt and pepper, cover and simmer until cauliflower is very tender, about 20 minutes. Add the sour cream and half and half and bring back to a very gentle simmer. Transfer soup to a blender (in batches) and puree until very smooth, then return to the pan to re-heat prior to serving.

Toast the baguette slices while the soup is re-warming, then spread thinly with the goat cheese and top with a little mound of caviar. Serve in shallow soup bowls, with a crouton floating on top of each. Drizzle generously with the truffle oil and some cracked pepper. Magic.

Pasta Fagioli
One big pot

There are a million versions of this soup, but this is Felix's favorite. He's addicted to any kind of beans, and will do just about anything for a good ham hock.

   3 cups fresh cranberry or borlotti beans (or 2 cups of dried…any white beans will do if
      truth be told)
   1 boiling potato peeled and cut into large pieces
   1 small ham hock
   9 cups chicken stock
   4 cups water
   6 tbsp olive oil
   I cup chopped sweet onion
   2 tsp crushed garlic
   1/4 cup finely chopped fresh Italian parsley
   2 tbsp tomato paste
   1 cup of pasta "rags" or any small pasta like ditalini or elbow macaroni.
   Grated Parmesan

If you have dried beans, soak them overnight in cold water and then drain them in the morning. If you have lucked out and found fresh beans, brilliant. Put the fresh or soaked beans, potato pieces and ham hock into a large soup pot, add 8 cups of the chicken stock and the water and simmer this very gently for about 1 1/4 hours, or until beans are tender. If you allow it to boil, the bean skins will crack and burst and we don't want burst beans do we?

Remove the ham hock and allow to cool. Pull off all the fatty skin and then take all the meat off the bone, shred and set aside. Give ham bone to dog, and discard the fat; Fido doesn't need love handles either.

Take half of the soup and puree in a blender until smooth than add back to the pot, along with the shredded meat. Keep the pot over low heat. In a sauté pan heat 2 tbsp of the olive oil and sauté the onions, garlic and parsley, until onions are soft and beginning to brown. Stir the tomato puree into the remaining 1 cup of chicken stock and add to the sauté pan. Pour the tomato base into the soup pot and stir to combine. You can make this soup a day ahead to this point and keep it in the fridge overnight. If you are pressing on however, add the pasta to the soup and cook gently until the pasta is tender. Turn off the heat and allow the soup to stand for 10 minutes before serving. Serve with the rest of the olive oil and the grated Parmesan over the top. (Olive oil is good fat, and wonderful for the complexion.)

Minestrone

One big pot

Easier than falling off a log, and a great way to get the fridge cleaned out. You can substitute winter veggies like carrots and potatoes during the colder months and asparagus instead of the beans, when it's in season. I have been known to put peas, red peppers, spinach and broccoli in too....it really works with anything.

2 tbsp olive oil
1 medium onion half chopped finely, half sliced
1 green pepper cut into 1" pieces
3 stalks celery chopped
1 green zucchini sliced into rings or chunks
1 yellow zucchini squash sliced into rings or chunks
1 cup chopped Italian green beans or any pole beans
1 14 oz can of chopped San Marzano tomatoes with juice
8 cups fat free low sodium chicken stock
1 cup dry white wine
1/4 cup chopped fresh Italian parsley
1/4 cup chopped fresh marjoram (or 1 tbsp dried)
2 small bay leaves
2 tbsp tomato paste
Piece of rind from Parmesan cheese (when you've grated all you can from a hunk of cheese, save rind in a baggie in the fridge)
1/2 tsp crushed red pepper flakes
1 bunch washed mustard greens roughly chopped (or kale or Swiss chard, whatever)
2 cups cooked whole wheat rigatoni
1 15 oz can cannellini beans (white kidney) rinsed
Fresh cracked black pepper
Fresh chopped basil, croutons and grated Parmesan for garnish

Heat the oil in a large heavy pot and sauté the onions, pepper and celery for a few minutes. Then add the zucchini, beans, tomatoes, chicken stock, wine, herbs, tomato paste, cheese rind, red pepper flakes, the washed greens and salt and pepper to taste. Bring this up to a boil, then put the lid on, turn it down to a simmer and let it go for an hour and a half. Stir it occasionally to keep things moving about evenly.

Just before you are ready to serve, put in the cooked rigatoni and the beans and let it simmer for another five or ten minutes. If you put the rigatoni in uncooked, it will soak up all the lovely juice and if you leave it in too long it will get too soft on you. Putting the beans in at the last minute also stops them from disintegrating. Serve with grated Parmesan and chopped fresh basil to sprinkle over the soup once served. If you are feeling energetic, toast up some Italian peasant bread, brushed with a little olive oil and garlic and topped with a little extra Parmesan. Definitely sexier with croutons.

Seafood Soup
One big pot

We are fortunate enough to live in the Pacific Northwest, and thus have access to beautiful seafood. It's important to make any dish like this with only the freshest stuff you can find otherwise you will not be happy. If you can't find really fresh seafood, make something else.

About these quantities; I find it completely impossible to make soup for two people, no matter how hard I try. Luckily, Felix will eat bowl after bowl of this stuff, so he is very helpful with my overproduction tendencies. Sensible people who are not afflicted with the same malady can of course cut these amounts down. These quantities will serve at least four (normal) people.

3 tbsp olive oil
1 tsp fennel seeds
1 large clove garlic crushed
1 fennel bulb sliced
1/2 sweet onion sliced
1 bunch scallions cleaned and chopped into 2" pieces
2 stalks celery
1 small zucchini
1/2 green pepper chopped
1/2 cup fresh chopped Italian parsley
1 bay leaf
1 tsp red pepper flakes
Fresh ground black pepper
1 cup dry white wine
5 cups chicken stock
1/4 cup tomato puree
1/2 cup chopped fresh basil
1 lb of firm fleshed white fish cut into large chunks (halibut, cod, monkfish etc.)
1/2 lb of medium shrimp peeled and de-veined
4 jumbo sea scallops halved

Dig out a large soup pot and heat the olive oil in it. Add the fennel seed and garlic and stir for a minute. Then add the fennel bulb, onion, scallions, celery, zucchini, green pepper, parsley, bay leaf, red pepper flakes and season with fresh cracked black pepper. Stir and fry the veggies for about 5 minutes until they're starting to brown and soften. Then add the white wine, the chicken stock and tomato puree. Stir well, cover and turn down to a simmer. Simmer like this for one hour. Then add the fish, shrimp and scallops gently, just pushing them under. Don't stir it about at all if you can help it, and don't allow the soup to boil either, otherwise, all the lovely chunks will disintegrate and you will have seafood mush. Just simmer until the seafood is all cooked through, about 10 minutes, and then serve with hot crusty bread.

If you like, you could also add some littleneck clams to this at the end. I usually cook the clams separately in a little white wine, parsley and garlic, just to make sure they all open and are fit to eat. Then I can take them out of the shells and dump into the soup. It's a lot easier to eat if you don't have to mess with the shells in your bowl of soup.

Felix's Cure-All Chicken Soup
One big pot

Now I will just mention that this is Felix's unabridged recipe, exactly as he made it for me; 100% man soup. If you want to keep the fat content down even further, you could use chicken breast meat instead of thighs, and also cool and de-fat the chicken cooking liquid in a fat separator, before you add it to the rest of the soup. Personally I think he did a marvelous job and it tastes fabulous this way.

> 6 chicken thighs, skin and excess fat removed
> 3 medium carrots washed and sliced into rounds
> 1 1/2 cups of onion roughly chopped
> 4 sticks of celery trimmed, cleaned and chopped (not fossilized)
> 2 bay leaves
> 1 small bunch of fresh thyme
> 3 tbsp olive oil
> 2 cloves garlic minced or crushed
> 1 large green pepper seeded and roughly chopped
> 49 ozs of low sodium, non fat chicken stock
> 1 or 2 large bunches of Kale, roughly chopped. (You can use cabbage or whatever greens
>   you like, but remove the tough stems and ribs before you chop.)
> 1 cup whole wheat pasta (rigatoni, rotelli, penne, whatever you fancy)
> Fresh cracked black pepper and grated Parmesan cheese to garnish.

Take your skinned and defatted thighs, (oh how I wish) 1 of the chopped carrots, half a cup of the chopped onion, 2 sticks of celery and 1 bay leaf and dump the lot into a large saucepan cover with cold water, add a little cracked black pepper and then bring it all to a boil. Immediately cover and reduce to a gentle simmer, and keep it there for at least an hour. When it's done, the chicken should be falling off the bones.

Once your chicken is meltingly tender, take off the heat and strain the liquid into a bowl (or your fat separator) and set aside. Let the chicken thighs cool, and then take all the meat off the bones and set this aside too. Discard the bones and the mushy vegetables from the strainer.

While your thighs are cooking, so to speak, grab a large soup pot and put the 3 tbsp of olive oil in it. Place over medium high heat and when hot, add the remaining onions, carrots and celery, and also add the bay leaf, thyme, chopped pepper and crushed garlic. Add a few grindings of cracked black pepper and stir this about for five minutes or so, then add the chicken stock and the chopped greens. Cover the pot and bring this up to a boil. When it reaches a boil, turn heat to medium low and settle it down to a simmer. Put in the reserved chicken meat, and cooking liquid and continue to simmer for at least an hour. The longer soup like this sits and simmers, the better it tastes. About half an hour before you want to eat, put the pasta into the soup and cook through.

When the pasta is tender, the soup is ready to serve. You can always add more stock if the pasta has soaked up too much liquid, and you like a soupier soup. Ladled into big bowls, with a generous sprinkle of Parmesan cheese on top, this stuff will cure anything.

Mulligatawny

For 4 (as a main course)

Not really and truly an Indian dish. I think English people invented it after getting kicked out of India. Whoever is responsible, it's delicious. You can also use any leftover cooked chicken (or turkey) for this soup instead of poaching the thighs and breast. If you don't want to use all the individual spices, you can use a blended curry powder; about 2 tbsp.

8 chicken thighs skinned and defatted
1 large boneless skinless chicken breast
2 tbsp olive oil
1 large onion chopped
2 stalks celery chopped
1 large jalapeno pepper seeded and very finely chopped
3/4 cup dried lentils (green, brown, yellow, whatever you fancy, rinsed and picked over)
1 tbsp ground coriander seeds
1 tbsp ground cumin seeds
1 tsp ground turmeric
1 tsp ground fenugreek seeds
2 bay leaves
6 cups non fat low sodium chicken broth
1 cup light coconut milk
Chopped fresh coriander (cilantro)

In a deep saucepan, poach the chicken in enough water to cover, over very gentle heat, until cooked through and tender… about an hour. Don't let it boil or the meat will get tough. (You can use extra chicken stock instead if you prefer.) Remove chicken from the poaching liquid, allow to cool, take the meat off the thigh bones and shred the breast meat.

Heat the olive oil in a large soup pot. Sauté the onion, celery and jalapeño until softened, about 3 minutes. Add the lentils, coriander, cumin, turmeric, fenugreek and bay leaves and stir it all about. Pour in the chicken stock and add the cooked chicken. Bring this to a boil then cover the pot and reduce to a slow simmer. Cook very gently for 1 1/2 hours then add the coconut milk and simmer for ten more minutes or so. Ladle into deep bowls and sprinkle with a little fresh coriander for garnish.

Split Pea & Ham with Tarragon
One big pot

Thick and green are not usually considered attractive attributes, but in the case of this soup, I think an exception must be made. It may take a while to make this soup, but it does not violate The Rule, because it is so mind numbingly simple. Make it on a rainy Sunday and use the long cooking times to do something useful, like nap.

> 2 cups dried split peas
> 2 large smoked ham hocks
> 2 tbsp olive oil
> 1 large onion finely chopped
> 10 cups non fat low sodium chicken stock
> 1 tbsp dried tarragon

Soak the split peas in plenty of cold water overnight. (Mega nap). The following morning, drain the peas and discard the soaking liquid. Put the ham hocks in a saucepan, cover with water and bring to a boil. Reduce the heat to low, cover the pan and cook until the meat is falling off the bones, about 2 hours. (Nap, or read about next vacation spot if you can stay awake.)

Remove the hocks from the water and cool. Once you can handle them, take all the meat off the bones, shred it and set aside. Discard the bones and fat, or make Fido a happy puppy again.

In a large soup pot, heat the oil to medium high and sauté the onion until just softened. Put in the reserved ham, the soaked peas, the stock and the tarragon. Bring to a boil, then cover the pot and simmer for about 1 1/2 hours. (Nap). Season with salt and pepper to taste. Crisp, baked garlic bread on the side is nice, if you're not too tired.

Gumbo
One big pot

"Who's your mama? Is she Catholic?" and "Can she make a roux?" I can't remember where I read or heard this but it has always tickled me. My Mum is not Catholic and wouldn't know a roux if it bit her, but despite my lack of authentic Cajun heritage, somehow, I still manage to make quite a decent Gumbo.

1 medium onion
3 stalks celery
1 green pepper
1/3 cup of oil
1/4 cup of flour
Fresh cracked black pepper
4 tbsp chopped fresh marjoram or oregano or 1 tsp of dried
A good sprig of fresh thyme or 1 tsp dried thyme
1 bayleaf
1 large can (8 cups) chicken stock
1 tbsp Worcestershire Sauce
1 24 oz can crushed tomatoes
1 large bag frozen chopped okra
1 tsp dried red pepper flakes or cayenne pepper
3 links hot Italian sausage cooked. (You can be very authentic and use Cajun sausage if
      you can get your hands on some)
2 small boneless skinless chicken breasts (you can use bone in thighs and drums if you
      want something to pick up and chew on.)
12 ozs lump crab meat (you can use legs and claws again if you want something to grab)
1/2 lb of large shrimp peeled and de-veined
File Gumbo
1 cup long grain brown rice

First of all finely chop the onion, celery and green pepper. Take the stem and seeds out of the pepper first. You should have roughly equal quantities of each. In a large heavy soup pot, heat the oil and then add the flour. (This is the roux part Mama is supposed to be good at). Keep the pot over fairly high heat and with a wooden spoon constantly stir it about. It will form a paste on the bottom of your pan. As this cooks, it will gradually get browner and browner, and this is what it is supposed to do. The desired result is quite a dark nutty brown color. Don't be faint of heart and give up when you only have golden or light brown. Be strong and hold out for nutty brown. Okay, once there, put in the chopped vegetables and stir about for a couple of minutes so they all get covered. Season with fresh, cracked black pepper. Now put in the herbs, the stock, the Worcestershire Sauce, the canned tomatoes, the okra and the pepper flakes. This will calm things down a bit, and when it comes back to a simmer, you can turn the heat down to very low and put a lid on it.

Sauté your chicken breasts, thighs or drummies in a little olive oil until just browned on the outside; they don't have to be entirely cooked through, then add to the pot. Slice the cooked sausage, and add to the pot. (I cook the sausages, whole, in the microwave) Now you can leave it to stew and evolve into something fabulous on the back burner. The longer you cook this stuff the better it is. I think two hours minimum is a good rule of thumb. If anything tries to get out during the cooking process, smack it sharply with the back of a wooden spoon and hold the lid down firmly until it gives up.

When you have left the gumbo alone, for as long as you can stand it, cook the rice in plenty of boiling salted water and drain through a sieve. You can then put the rice in a serving dish and keep it warm at this point, because the seafood only takes a second or two to cook through.

Toss the peeled and de-veined shrimp into the gumbo pot, stir, and wait 5 minutes. Then gently, very gently indeed, add the crab meat. Don't stir it about or the crab will disintegrate and be lost to you forever. Just let it warm through for about 10 more minutes over low heat and it's ready to serve.

The idea is to spoon however much rice you want into the bottom of a large soup bowl, then the Gumbo is ladled over the top and liberally sprinkled with the File. Just FYI, day old, re-heated Gumbo is even more fantastic.

Halibut Sweet Potato Chowder

For 4 (as a main course)

I saw a recipe for something like this in a magazine in my doctor's waiting room and I thought it looked really good. I was about to get my stubborn wrinkles re-Botoxed, and was magazine flipping to take my mind off the needles that are necessarily involved in that process. Anyway, not wanting to be crass, (or caught) I refrained from ripping the page out of the magazine, and tried to memorize the ingredients. Unfortunately, having needles stuck in your face is terrible for the short term memory, and the only things I remembered later were Halibut and Sweet Potato. So, I made something up, and it's not bad at all. Maybe I should have called this one Botox Broth, I'll ask Nancy. (See Crimp Cakes.)

> 3 tbsp olive oil
> 1 large onion sliced
> 2 large sweet potatoes peeled and chunked into 1 inch cubes
> 2 tsp crushed garlic
> 2 fully cooked, spicy chicken sausages sliced (or any spicy sausage you like)
> 2 tsp ground turmeric
> 1 tsp hot pepper flakes (or to your taste)
> Fresh cracked black pepper to taste.
> 1 49 oz can of non fat low sodium chicken broth
> 1 cup non fat sour cream
> 1/2 lb of asparagus trimmed and cut into 1" lengths (green beans and zucchini work too)
> 12 large firm Roma tomatoes diced
> 1 lb nice thick, halibut fillet, skinned and cut into large chunks

Heat the olive oil in a nice wide soup pot with a heavy bottom (I sympathize I really do). When hot, put in onion, sweet potato and garlic, and stir about a bit until the onion starts to soften and get golden, turn the heat down a bit if it gets a bit too excited. Now toss in the sausage slices, the turmeric, hot pepper and black pepper. Stir to coat all the stuff and then pour in the chicken broth. Put a lid on the pot and leave it to simmer gently until the sweet potato chunks are tender, about 20 minutes. Some will disintegrate a bit, especially if you're an enthusiastic stirrer, but this gives a lovely creaminess to the soup which, personally, I like.

After the twenty minutes or so, stir in the sour cream and add the asparagus and tomato. Stir this about until all is combined and then pop the halibut chunks on top. Push the chunks gently under the surface so they get all covered with the soup and also they cook more evenly that way. Cover the pot again and leave to simmer very gently until the halibut is just cooked through, about 10 – 15 minutes. Don't let it boil vigorously or all the halibut will disintegrate.

My Mum's Beef Stew with Dumplings
For 4 (with maybe a few leftovers)

Truly the stuff of my childhood. Simple, peasant food, and so good it makes you forget you're not supposed to eat root vegetables because they spike the blood sugar, blah blah blah.......sometimes you just have to say "bite me" don't you? Anyway, you can use any combination of veggies that you like, sweet potato, yams, regular potato, carrots etc. Whatever grabs you will work fine. Just plan on about 8 or 9 cups of shredded vegetables; it cooks down quite a bit. You'll need an industrial strength grater for this, and a steady hand so that you don't add your knuckles to the mix. It's supposed to be beef stew, not knuckle soup.

> 1 large yam
> 1 medium turnip
> 2 cups grated Hubbard squash
> 1 large parsnip
> 1 large sweet onion
> 2 tbsp olive oil
> 1 lb lean chuck steak cut into 1" cubes
> 49 oz can of non fat, low sodium chicken stock
> 1 cup biscuit mix (like Bisquick.) (Or you can use a roll of those ready to bake biscuits,
>   just pop the can open and slip them onto the top of your stew.)

Peel the yam, turnip, squash and parsnip and coarsely grate. Leave a few chunks of each vegetable to give some chunkier texture to the stew. This will also save you from shredding your knuckles trying to grate the last bits. Peel and chop the onion and set all the vegetables aside. Put the olive oil into a very large soup pot over medium high heat. When the oil is hot, sauté the steak cubes until browned all over. You may have to do this in batches. When the meat is brown, remove from the pan and set aside. Put all the chopped and grated vegetables into the pot and add the stock. Now, put the meat back in along with any accumulated juices. Bring to a boil and then cook, covered, over low heat, for at least 1 1/2 hours preferably longer, you can't overdo it really. Season with salt and pepper to taste.

Mix the biscuit mix according to the package instructions and shape into 8 small dumplings. Pop the dumplings into the stew and push gently under. They will swell up quite a bit. Don't stir the stew much after this or you'll break up the dumplings, just gently scrape the bottom and stir under them now and again. Keep the pot on very low heat and there should be no problem. The dumplings will take about another 20 to 25 minutes to cook through. Then just ladle into bowls and overeat, like I did last night. You'll never guess what I weighed this morning.

Kitchen Sink Soup (AKA Winter White Soup)
One big pot

The prototype of this soup was constructed with whatever happened to be in the fridge/pantry/freezer on an afternoon when I got something in my eye and couldn't see going to the grocery store to get dinner. Everything but the kitchen sink went in........hence the ugly name........It turned out to be mostly white, hence the more attractive alternative.

    2 tbsp olive oil
    1 large onion peeled and chopped
    2 sticks celery
    1 head cauliflower cut into small chunks
    1 large russet potato peeled and cut into small chunks
    10 cups non fat low sodium chicken broth
    3/4 cup orzo (or any kind of pasta you like)
    1 large can white cannellini beans (low sodium, with juice)
    1 cup non fat sour cream

In a large soup pot heat the oil over medium high heat, then sauté the onion, celery, cauliflower and potato pieces for several minutes, or until a few brown spots appear on the cauliflower. Add the chicken stock and bring to a boil. Turn heat down to low, cover the pot and simmer for about 1 1/2 hours. Stir it about occasionally and the cauliflower and potato will break down just enough to give it a bit of thickness. Add the orzo and the beans with their juice, and continue to cook until the orzo is done. Then stir in the sour cream and warm through. Serve with nice crusty bread for a very satisfying experiment.

# Salads...

Perhaps Mexico doesn't immediately make one think of great salads, but I really have had some great ones there. Strangely, chicken livers spring to mind.....

Mexico

We love Mexico. We can't go there anymore, because Felix has a tendency to insult people in Spanish. No seriously, we really can't go there because we get horribly sick every time we set foot on Mexican soil. No one else does, just Felix and me........mostly me actually.

We loved Mexico so much that every year we'd make plans to keep ourselves healthy so we could keep going back. Oh the promises we made.....No more beach restaurants, we will wash every vegetable we eat in undiluted bleach, we'll stay at the most expensive hotel in town and only eat there! None of it worked. By the time I was on a first name basis with the local doctor, we realized that we had to vacation somewhere else. Normal people get shots before they go on vacation, I would get mine during vacation, without fail. **"Hi Dr. Alejandro." "Hi Antonia, has it been a year already? Now where would you like your shot, arm or butt?"** So polite.......lovely people.

Although not the reason we can't go back, Felix actually did insult a few people while we were in Mexico........unintentionally of course. He was really keen to learn Spanish, but found it very challenging. His brain, while extremely good at math and complex legal problems, turns to mush when faced with foreign languages...... including English. So..... keen as he was, Spanish was a bit of a problem.

We bought tapes to listen to in the car, which helped me quite a bit, but drove Felix to distraction, and also into the ditch several times. He'd weave along the freeway at 30 mph alternately butchering Spanish pronunciation and swearing like a longshoreman. So, for the safety of our fellow motorists, the tapes had to go. After the tapes, we tried speaking Spanish to each other every day........our exchanges usually went something like this:

Me: **"Como estas mi amor?"** (how are you my love)

Felix: **"Estoy mooey wapo!"** (I am very handsome) (and obviously very modest too!)

Felix: **"How do you say, I'd like a martini in Spanish?"**

Me: **"Yo quiero un Martini I think."**

Felix: **"Great. Yo quiero un Martini then."**

We usually ran out of Spanish conversation after that, and by the time we tried it again, he would have forgotten how to say I'd like a Martini. And so it went. Yo slogged on alone, intent on mastering at least the basics before my next trip to Dr. Alejandro; I thought it would be nice to be able to request my shot in the butt in Spanish. Eventually, I learned enough to be able to exchange a few pleasantries, or shop for groceries, and Felix learned enough to insult people, or reduce them to hysterical giggles.

I warned him about the obvious pitfalls in Spanish, but to no avail. Sitting in a little bar one evening, Felix went right ahead and asked the gentleman to his left, how many anuses he had instead of how old he was. We weren't thrown out, but several people sustained minor injuries after falling off their barstools.

That put him off Spanish for a couple of days, but he soon got his nerve back and was at it again. We were sunning ourselves by the pool at our hotel, and Felix decided a second round of Margaritas was in order. As usual, he asked me how to order them in Spanish. Fearing another insult to some poor unsuspecting Mexican citizen, I refused to tell him, and begged him to speak English. Undeterred by my lack of cooperation, he wandered off muttering **"Yo quiero"** something or other. After a couple of minutes, hysterical laughter wafted up from the bar below. I darted downstairs to find the two bartenders in hysterics. **"What did you say"** I hissed. **"Nothing…..well….I don't know actually"**, Felix grumbled. When the bartenders regained their composure they informed me, between giggles, that Felix told them he'd been snorkeling tomorrow, and had seen a chicken. I think he probably meant to say pulpo for octopus, but who knows with Felix. Today, tomorrow, pollo pulpo, whatever. At least there was no intimate anatomy involved this time.

So lately we've been giving the wonderful people of Mexico a break, and have been vacationing in the Caribbean instead. Lots of French spoken in the Caribbean, but so far……….. not so much as a Oui out of Felix.

Panzanella

Makes a big bowl full…..squint at the ingredients and imagine!

Bread salad…..Yikes! Just uttering those words slaps 2lbs on each thigh, so I recommend that you keep this for special occasions, when there are lots of other people around to help you eat it. Strong, lean, people, with no fear of carbohydrates.

> 6 cups half inch cubes of coarse Italian peasant bread
> 8 ripe medium sized tomatoes chopped into half inch pieces
> 1 English cucumber chopped into half inch pieces (no need to peel)
> 1 large sweet onion cut in half and then into 1/4 inch thick slices
> 1 large red pepper seeded and coarsely chopped
> 1 cup loosely packed basil torn into pieces
> 1/3 cup extra virgin olive oil
> 1/4 cup good quality red wine vinegar
> 1/2 tsp crushed garlic
> 1/2 tsp Dijon mustard
> Sea salt and fresh black pepper to taste

The bread must be the coarse Italian type, and preferably day old. Toast the cubes of bread in a 350 degree oven for about 15 minutes, or pop it under the broiler for a few moments, just to toast it up a little, give it a little color on the edges.

Put the first six ingredients in a large bowl and gently mix together. Cover with cling wrap and allow this mixture to sit for at least an hour to let all the flavors mingle properly. About half an hour before you are ready to serve the salad, combine the oil vinegar, garlic and mustard in a jar and shake until combined, pour this over the salad, season with salt and pepper and gently toss.

This is truly dynamite the next day…… usually fought over with great gusto.

Israeli Couscous Salad

See previous recipe

Lots of people I have met seem to be unfamiliar with Israeli couscous, and I can only imagine that this is because they don't haunt Middle Eastern grocery stores the way I do. They have such exotic (and sometimes dangerous looking) foods that I am just fascinated to the point of gobsmacked. Anyway, this Israeli Couscous stuff looks a bit like Tapioca or, more unfortunately, dried frog spawn, but it is, actually, just plain old pasta in yet another shape. It's a bit like my selection of black pants actually, basically the same stuff, but in an infinite number of shapes and sizes……. and any woman worth her hormones knows how important the different sizes are.

> 2 medium tomatoes halved
> 2 cups Israeli couscous
> 1 bunch scallions cleaned and chopped
> 1 red pepper seeded and chopped
> 1/2 cup currants
> 1/2 cup pine nuts
> 1/2 cup capers
> 1/4 cup chopped cilantro
> 1/4 cup chopped fresh basil
> Zest of 1 small lemon
> 1 tbsp lemon juice
> 1 tbsp sherry vinegar
> 2 tbsp good olive oil
> 1/2 tsp hot pepper flakes
> Fresh cracked black pepper

Heat the oven to 325 degrees and roast the tomatoes for an hour. When they are done, remove from oven and let cool.

While the tomatoes are roasting, cook the couscous in plenty of boiling water until al dente. Drain through a sieve and run under cold water to stop the cooking. Turn the couscous into a mixing bowl and stir in the scallions, red pepper, currants, pine nuts, capers, cilantro, basil and lemon zest.

To make the dressing slip the skins off the tomatoes and discard, put the flesh in a blender with the lemon juice, sherry vinegar, olive oil and pepper flakes, then add 1 tbsp water. Blend until smooth. Taste and adjust seasoning if necessary, then pour over salad and toss gently until the dressing is distributed evenly.

If I want to make this into a whole meal in the summertime, I add loads of cold, cooked crab, shrimp, scallops and calamari and serve it on top. Mound it up on a huge platter with fresh lemon wedges and butter lettuce all around the edge.

Southwestern Caesar Salad
For 4 – 6 (depends how hungry your people are)

You could serve this as an appetizer salad with some jalapeño hush puppies too I think, or maybe as a side salad with crimp cakes for a light dinner.

1/4 cup non fat sour cream
2 tbsp egg beaters
2 tbsp fresh lemon juice
2 tbsp red wine vinegar
Dash of Worcestershire sauce
1/2 tsp whole grain mustard
1 large garlic clove peeled and crushed
2 anchovies finely chopped
2 tbsp of olive oil
1/4 cup shallots finely chopped
1/4 cup chopped fresh cilantro
2 tbsp canned chopped fire roasted green chilics or jalapeños
1 bag Romaine lettuce or 1 head washed, spun dry and torn into pieces
1/2 red pepper chopped
1 large fresh corn cob with kernels removed
1 cup cherry tomatoes halved
1/2 cup grated Parmesan cheese
1 cup croutons
Fresh black pepper

Put the first 12 ingredients into a very large screw top jar or a bowl with a tight fitting lid; shake vigorously until all is combined. Put lettuce and remaining ingredients into a large salad bowl and dress with just enough dressing to coat. Toss well, add some more black pepper and serve.

Mushroom Fennel & Parmesan Salad

For 4

This is a very simple and elegant appetizer salad that I had at a dinner party once. I was wowed because I thought the combination was really spectacular and it's EASY! I didn't even have to ask for the recipe.

Three things to remember: 1) You need a mandoline to slice things extra extra paper thin, 2) the mushrooms and fennel must be daisy fresh and 3) you have to make this just minutes before you serve it. It is an impatient salad, and does not wait around well.

> 4 very fresh, large white mushrooms
> 1 small very fresh fennel bulb, tough outer bits removed and base trimmed
> A block of good quality Parmesan
> 1 tbsp capers
> 2 tbsp extra virgin olive oil
> 2 tbsp fresh lemon juice
> 2 tbsp chopped chives
> Fresh cracked black pepper
> White truffle oil

Wipe the mushrooms clean with a damp cloth, don't get them too wet whatever you do. With the mandoline set on a very thin cut, slice the mushrooms, the fennel bulb and Parmesan in approximately equal amounts. The slices need to be paper thin, almost see through in fact. Put the mushroom and fennel slices in a bowl and toss with the capers, virgin olive oil, lemon juice and chives. Divide these slices between four salad plates then top with the Parmesan slices. You can drizzle more olive oil and lemon juice over each if you like more dressing. Now just give each a good grind of black pepper and few drops of white truffle oil over the top and serve immediately.

Spinach Arugula Candied Walnuts Gorgonzola & Pear Salad
For 4 (as an appetizer)

Even hardened carnivores will usually eat this one. It's the blue cheese you see. I think it's probably possible to eat an old tennis shoe with enough Gorgonzola on it.

> 1/4 cup brown sugar
> 1/3 cup water
> 1/2 cup walnut halves
> 1 large shallot finely chopped
> 2 rashers of very lean bacon
> 1 tsp roasted garlic
> 2 tbsp sherry vinegar
> 1 generous tsp honey
> 3 tbsp olive oil
> 2 cups baby spinach leaves
> 2 cups arugula
> 1 firm but ripe pear cored and cut into thin wedges
> 1/2 cup crumbled Gorgonzola. Maytag Blue or Point Reyes Blue are also lovely choices.

Pre-heat the oven to 375 degrees. Put the sugar and water in a saucepan and dissolve the sugar over medium high heat. Put the walnuts into the sugar water and bring to a boil. Simmer for 5 minutes and then remove nuts with a slotted spoon and put onto a baking sheet lined with non-stick foil. Pop them into the oven and bake for about 8 to 10 minutes. They should get nice and brown and crisp. Once done, let the walnuts cool and set aside. Don't burn these little pups, if you turn your back for a second too long, they're toast....well actually, burnt toast.

In a non stick sauté pan fry the shallots and bacon together until shallots are golden and bacon is browned and crisp. The bacon will give off enough fat so you don't have to add any other oil. Put the garlic, sherry vinegar and honey, into a screw top jar and shake well until blended. Add the shallots and bacon, season with salt and pepper and shake again.

Put the spinach and arugula in a large salad bowl toss in the pear slices and the candied walnuts and sprinkle the blue cheese over the top. Drizzle just enough dressing over to lightly coat. Add a little black pepper, then toss the salad and serve.

Composed Baby Greens with Prosciutto & Breadsticks
For 2 (as an appetizer)

Now this is dead easy, and only involves assembly, which, in my opinion is a highly desirable quality in a recipe, but it is different, so it still gets you a lot of extra points. Quite why it impresses people so much, I don't know, maybe it's the fact that food doesn't often stand up on its own. Whatever, as long as it does, I shall keep taking the credit for being a lot better in the kitchen than I really am.

1 blood orange (half a small pink grapefruit will do if you can't find a blood orange)
2 tbsp olive oil
1 tsp balsamic vinegar
2 cups mixed baby lettuces
1/2 red, yellow or orange pepper very thinly sliced lengthwise
1/4 cup lightly toasted pecans roughly chopped (10 minutes in a 375 degree oven will do)
2 tbsp crumbled Feta cheese
2 long slices of paper thin prosciutto
2 long thin breadsticks
2 cocktail sticks/toothpicks

First thing to do is make the dressing. Cut the blood orange in half, lengthwise not across the segments, and squeeze the juice from one half of the orange into a screw top jar. To this, add the olive oil and balsamic vinegar and shake well.

Peel the other half of the blood orange and pull off all the membranes that you can, then cut the flesh into little bites. Put the washed greens in a mixing bowl and add the pepper strips, pecans, Feta and the orange pieces. Now for the fiddly bit. Lay one of the slices of prosciutto on your work surface and arrange half of the mixed salad on it. Wrap the prosciutto around it to hold it all together, and secure the ends with a toothpick. Set upright in the middle of your salad plate. You might need to fan it out a bit so the salad greens drape nicely out over the girdle of prosciutto. Just fiddle with it until it stands to attention. Give your salad dressing another shake and then drizzle it over and around the salad. Lastly, take the breadsticks and break each in two, and then stick them decoratively into the upright salad. Don't forget to remind people about the toothpicks or you could end up with some unintentional piercings.

Insalata Caprese
For 2 -3

This is the only Italian I can speak, which is a shame really as it's such a beautiful language for yelling in. Felix thinks he knows a few phrases, but as he is not entirely sure what they mean, I try to dissuade him from using them in public. Buffalo Mozzarella is the best to use for this, but if buffalos are in short supply in your neighborhood, then that made from humble cows milk will do nicely.

    2 large ripe tomatoes
    1 ball fresh Mozzarella packed in water
    Fresh basil washed and dried
    Extra virgin olive oil for drizzling
    Balsamic vinegar for drizzling

Two or three of these stacks are sufficient for an appetizer portion, depending on the size of your tomatoes. Try to match the diameter of the Mozzarella slices to the diameter of the tomato slices and use your own judgment on how many to make per person.

Slice the tomatoes into 1/4 inch thick slices and top with a 1/4 inch thick slice of Mozzarella. On top of each piece of cheese lay a small, whole basil leaf. Now drizzle with good quality olive oil and just a few drops of balsamic vinegar here and there. Last but not least, crack fresh black pepper all over the top and serve.

Salade Niçoise
For 2

Felix and I have been to France a few times, and I must say we've found no indication whatsoever that the French are getting any friendlier......certainly not in Paris anyway. They do incredible things with food though, and they're intimidatingly stylish too......and the women are thin and gorgeous and there's the perfume and the fashion houses........the effortless decor, the palaces and gardens...... You know, for people with so much going for them, you'd think they could be a bit more friendly to the rest of us plebs.

> 4 whole leaves of red leaf lettuce washed and dried
> 2 ripe tomatoes sliced
> 1/2 green pepper thinly sliced
> 2 radishes sliced
> 12 whole green beans steamed until just tender crisp
> 8 hard boiled quail eggs halved lengthwise
> 6 anchovies
> 1 6 oz can of best quality tuna packed in olive oil
> 1/4 cup Niçoise olives
> 2 tbsp olive oil
> 1 tbsp red wine vinegar
> Chopped fresh chives and lemon wedges for garnish

Place two lettuce leaves on each plate and then build from the outside in and up, layer the tomatoes, pepper, radishes and green beans, arrange the quail eggs and anchovies strategically around, and put half of the drained tuna in the middle of each stack. Scatter the olives over the top.

Whisk together the oil and vinegar and drizzle half over each salad. Top with the chopped chives and some fresh ground black pepper. Squeeze lemon juice over and voila!

Crab Shrimp Apple & Gorgonzola Salad
with Green Herb Dressing
For 2 (hungry people)

This is downright delicious, and lovely for a hot summer evening, because it doesn't involve sweating over a hot stove. Summer evenings are not the time to be sweating over anything......... no wait, I would certainly make an exception for a hot date.

The recipe is a cross between a main dish salad served at our favorite local Italian restaurant, and a sumptuous seafood salad my friend Kitty has bragging rights to. As she so rightly points out, "assembly only" cookery frees the cook from the shackles of the stove and allows for proper appreciation of cocktail hour.

The following amounts may seem like a lot, but Felix and I can polish this off, in one sitting, without batting an eyelid. Feel free to reduce the amount of crab and shrimp if you are more restrained eaters. The extra dressing can be stored in the fridge for a few days, and is really good on just about anything...... baked fish or chicken, in sandwiches, on baked potatoes and other salads, or as a dip for veggies.

For the Salad
1/2 cup pecans
Salad greens for two (You can use whatever, romaine, mixed greens, spinach etc.)
1 nice crunchy apple, not too sweet, not too sharp (Braeburn maybe)
1 cup cherry or grape tomatoes
1/3 cup crumbled Gorgonzola cheese
1 large avocado
Juice of half a lemon
1/2 lb of lump crab meat
1/2 pound of gently boiled shrimp, peeled and de-veined
Lemon wedges

For the Green Herb Dressing
1/4 cup of chopped fresh basil
1 tbsp of chopped fresh Italian parsley
1/4 cup of chopped fresh cilantro
1/4 cup of non fat mayonnaise
1/4 cup non fat sour cream
1/2 an avocado peeled and chopped
1 clove garlic crushed
Juice of 1 large lemon
2 tbsp white wine vinegar
2 tbsp water
Fresh cracked black pepper

First thing to do is spread the pecans on a baking sheet and toast them in a 375 degree oven for about 10 minutes. Just until they are nice and crisp, but be careful not to burn them. Remove from the oven and set aside to cool. When cool, roughly chop them. While the pecans are toasting, make the green herb dressing. Put all the ingredients in a blender and give it a whirl until it's that lovely green goddess color.

Mound the washed salad greens onto a large flat serving platter, or if you prefer, you can build individual salads on dinner plates, the same construction procedure applies. This also discourages dipping in for seconds, which I'm afraid I'm very prone to doing if not watched carefully.

Quarter and core the apple, and then cut into thin sticks, like matchsticks, and sprinkle over the greens. Halve the cherry or grape tomatoes and add them too. Pick over the lump crab meat, to make sure there is no shell in it, then drape the crab and the shrimp seductively over the greens. Halve the avocado lengthwise and remove the pit. Get the skin off it, cut the flesh into large chunks and add to your salad. Crumble the Gorgonzola over the top, and sprinkle with the toasted pecans.

Lastly, take a few spoonfuls of the green herb dressing, and pour/dollop/drizzle over the top of the whole thing. Everyone has their own idea of how much dressing is the right amount, so this is another reason to build individual salads. Fresh cracked black pepper and lemon wedges to squeeze over all are essential.

Grilled Shrimp Avocado & Pink Grapefruit Salad

For 2 (for a light lunch maybe)

As fresh, and good for you, as a new coat of "Mademoiselle" polish on your toe nails.

- 4 tbsp olive oil
- 1 tsp hot red pepper flakes
- Fresh cracked black pepper
- 12 jumbo shrimp peeled and de-veined
- 3 cups wild mixed baby greens
- 1/2 of a small ruby grapefruit peeled and sectioned
- 1 small ripe avocado peeled, pitted and cut into small chunks
- 1/2 cup sweet corn kernels
- 2 tbsp sherry vinegar
- 1 tbsp fresh chopped cilantro

Put the shrimp in a bowl and toss with 2 tbsp of the olive oil and the red and black peppers.....make sure they're all nicely coated. Cook shrimp on a grill until just tender or you can use a sauté pan or a broiler.....whatever is easiest. Just don't overcook them. When they are done to your liking, cool them to room temperature.

While shrimp are cooking, put the greens into a large bowl and peel all the skin off the grapefruit segments, so all you have is the actual grapefruit flesh, then cut the segments into bite sized pieces and add to the greens. Add 3/4 of the chunks of avocado to the greens and also the sweet corn. Mash the remaining 1/4 of the avocado.

In a small glass jar with a lid, put the sherry vinegar, cilantro, 2 tbsp olive oil, the mashed avocado and shake it all about until it's well blended. Pour over the greens mixture and toss well, season with fresh cracked black pepper and toss again. Divide between two plates and put the grilled shrimp on the top.

Chicken Liver Salad with Crispy Leeks
For 2

Strange but true, but before we got banned from Mexico, Felix and I had the best chicken liver salad I have ever tasted, at a little café in Huatulco.....and not a tortilla in sight. It's a lunch size sort of salad, and this is how I (sort of) remember it.

> 6 tbsp olive oil
> 1 small tender leek sliced into thin rounds or very thin strips and very well washed.
> 3 cups baby mixed greens
> 1/2 red bell pepper seeded and very finely chopped
> 6 cherry tomatoes halved
> 1/3 cup Feta cheese crumbled
> 8 - 10 chicken livers trimmed of fat, rinsed and patted dry
> 1 tbsp regular balsamic vinegar
> 1 tsp honey
> Some extra old, very fine Balsamic vinegar for drizzling (should be good and thick)

In a large sauté pan, heat 2 tbsp of the olive oil over medium high heat. Separate out the individual rings or strips of the leek then sauté until nicely browned; some crispy edges are nice. Remove your crispy leeks from the pan and set aside to cool on some paper towel.

Put the salad greens into a large bowl and add the red pepper, the tomatoes and the Feta cheese.

Heat another 2 tbsp olive oil in sauté pan and sauté the chicken livers until just cooked through, they should still be slightly pink on the inside. About 7 to 8 minutes.

While the livers are cooking, in a small glass jar with a screw top shake the regular balsamic vinegar, the remaining 2 tbsp of olive oil and the honey. When well blended, pour over the salad greens, season with fresh black pepper and toss well. Divide the salad greens between two plates and then place half of the sautéed chicken livers on each. Top with the crispy leeks and drizzle some of the very fine old balsamic vinegar over the top of it all.

Flank Steak & Wild Rice Salad

For 2

Hearty diet food; guaranteed to stick to your ribs as they say. You can use tame rice and less of it if you prefer, but Felix gets a bit wobbly if he doesn't get his carbs.

1 small flank steak
1/4 cup low sodium soy sauce
1/4 cup Worcestershire sauce
2 tsp crushed garlic
3/4 cup wild rice
1 tbsp mayonnaise
1 tbsp non fat sour cream
1 tbsp prepared horseradish
1 tbsp water
1 tsp whole grain Dijon type mustard
1 tbsp lemon juice
1 bag mixed wild greens
12 grape tomatoes
1/2 cup crumbled blue cheese
1 14 oz can quartered artichoke hearts drained and gently squeezed dry
1 bunch scallions washed trimmed and chopped

Trim your flank steak of all fat, then pop into a gallon sized baggie. Toss in the soy sauce, Worcestershire sauce and half the garlic and shake it all around to cover the meat. Pop this back into the fridge and let stew for at least two hours, the longer the better, but it will still be good after two hours. Patience is indeed a virtue but lord knows it's not always available in my house.

Cook the wild rice in plenty of boiling water. Drain, rinse in cool water and set aside to cool completely. Make the dressing by putting mayo, sour cream, horseradish, water, remaining garlic, mustard and lemon juice in a screw top glass jar and shaking vigorously. Heat the grill and cook flank steak for about 3 to 4 minutes per side for rare, or you can grill under the broiler or sauté in a large pan, whatever seems like a good idea at the time. While the steak is grilling, toss the greens, tomatoes, blue cheese, artichoke hearts and scallions in a large salad bowl. Scatter the cool rice over the top of the salad and pop back into the fridge to stay cold.

When the steak is done to your liking. Take off the grill and allow to rest for 5 minutes before slicing. While the meat rests, pour dressing over the salad, season with black pepper and toss gently. Slice the steak across the grain into 1/2" thick strips and arrange them over the top of the salad. Extra horseradish on the side is a good idea.

Fish & Seafood...

We've had some of the most wonderful seafood on the Friendly Island. Give me grouper at least 3 days a week and I'll show you a happy camper.

St. Martin

Currently at about 30,000 feet I think, and enjoying a surprisingly good Bloody Mary. Thank god for frequent flyer miles, because I do love first class. I know it's snotty of me, and I'll probably burn in hell for it, but the best thing about flying first class is the part where people walk though the cabin on their way back to the coach section and lust after your first class seat. I did the cool blonde, rich bitch impression today.........intellectual novel in one hand, (trashy one I'm actually reading stowed under seat in front) Bloody Mary in the other hand, slightly bored expression........no eye contact of course, and voila! All that practice in the bathroom mirror has really paid off, and the fact that I'm not really blonde anymore doesn't seem to have affected my performance at all. Hopefully coach class was suitably impressed. Oooh I'm going to burn, I really am. Perhaps if I knit woolly hats for the homeless, or put in a few hours at a soup kitchen, when I get home, I could plea bargain for a couple weeks in purgatory, instead of eternity in hell.

Anyway, speaking of food..... I'm feeling pretty smug that I'm having a healthy breakfast.......lots of vegetables in a Bloody Mary.........tomato juice, celery and ....Vodka, which is made from potatoes, and last time I checked, potatoes were vegetables so.....I think I'm still okay there. Apparently I could have had something calling itself a sausage quesadilla, to go along with the Bloody Mary, but the thought of all that white carbohydrate and animal fat clinging to my butt, was just too much to bear, and I was able to staunchly refuse. Felix will need help with his anyway. No calories in other people's food.

We're on our way home from a fabulous two weeks on the island of St. Martin, and Felix is not a happy puppy. He has an extremely bad case of the going home blues, and while I've been entertaining myself tormenting the coach passengers, he's been gazing out the window and moaning quietly.......... at least the wracking sobs have subsided now.

Personally, I'm not too depressed about returning to the real world, particularly as I now have a nicely tanned bottom. My first since about the age of three I believe. Felix finally talked me into a thong, and I must say I'm glad..... because brown fat definitely looks better than white fat. Perhaps I should have had that sausage thingy after all. I was terribly reluctant about the thong business at first....... after all I'm not 20 anymore, not even times two....ouch......... and I didn't want to scare the locals or anything, but after a couple of stiff Margaritas, on a very quiet beach and with a firm grip on my safety sarong, I actually bared my ivory buns to the world.....not ivory hard alas, but definitely ivory white. There were some fairly vivid shades of red and pink on the way to golden brown, but only Felix saw that part, and he's color blind anyway, so it wasn't really an issue.

We did have a smashing time though.......from the time we got off the plane from Seattle, to the time I dragged him kicking and screaming back to the airport, it was two weeks of sheer bliss. We touched down at Princess Juliana airport, with sunshine everywhere and Felix beaming from ear to ear. I managed to prevent him from doing a Pope impression, and kissing the ground as he got off the plane, but he did plant quite a smacker on the immigration officer........the man was a good sport though, and didn't have us arrested or anything.

We rented a cute cottage on the French side of the island, complete with pool, ocean view, tons of Bougainvillea and complete privacy. The villa company sent a nice lady to welcome us, but she didn't stay long....... I think it might have been Felix's standard arrival routine that spooked her........... First of all he investigates the fridge for beer or wine, then he tears off all his clothing, and hits the pool. Felix is not really an exhibitionist, he just gets a bit over excited in the sun. (I bet she remembers him next year....... well bits of him anyway.)

When Felix had settled down a bit, we ventured out to the local deli for staples. I swear, I would give up my last ounce of Crème de la Mér for a deli like this at home; duck breasts, frogs legs, truffles, caviar, smoked salmon, quail eggs, pâté, pastries, a chocolaterie AND a splendid wine cellar. This was total sensory overload for Felix and me.......so, after a lot of hyperventilating and about $200, we piled back into our tiny car with our booty and headed for home. It was getting dark, but fortunately, Felix is an accomplished St. Martin driver, and he quickly picked up on the local rules of the road again......there are only two after all: (1) Speed above 80 mph at all times unless attempting to park, and then 50 is acceptable, and (2) make no eye contact with other drivers until you have executed your illegal move, then smile and wave.

After our fine picnic, washed down with plenty of well chilled Pouilly Fuissé, we retired to bed for a good night's sleep........or in my case a good hour's sleep, after which I was dragged from the gentle arms of Morpheus by a raucous chorus of cicadas, several unidentified things galloping across the roof, and a banana palm trying its level best to get in the bedroom window. It was blowing a hooley out there. I tossed and turned for a while, kicked Felix a bit to see if he would wake up and keep me company, (not a chance) and eventually headed for the sofa and my book. The trashy one of course.

At about two o'clock, Felix staggered out, squinted at me, and then, satisfied that I was not in any immediate danger, or worse, drinking the rest of the Pouilly Fouissé, he shuffled back to bed to resume his slumbers. I swear the man can drop off during an Aerosmith concert if he wants to. Two more hours, and several chapters of serial killer/grisly murders later, the eyes were drooping, I didn't give a hoot whether the banana palm got in or not, and Morpheus took me back.

Once we got used to the nightly roof races and the banana palm beating on the window, things went mostly to plan..............There was plenty of great French food, lots of lying around in the sun, and of course, Margaritas for breakfast. Well they do come in the same health category as Bloody Marys because they're also chock full of fruits and veggies. It's true..... lime juice from limes, triple sec from oranges, and tequila from cacti. I'm not sure if cacti come under fruits or vegetables, but they must be one or the other for goodness sake. Anyway, it was fabulous, but over too quickly, and here we are on the way back to Seattle and rain.

I think Felix is cheering up a bit though, even the whimpering has stopped, so he's probably already planning our next escape to sun, sea and sand. He'll be a bit fragile for a few weeks though, so I must do something nice to cheer him up when we get home……. (Note to self: purchase sandbox, faux palm tree, tanning bed and at least three cases of Pouilly Fouissé stat.)

Crab Stuffed Shrimp with Tamarind Mango Sauce
For 2

This might sound a bit fiddly, but it's really not that much work and it is pretty delish. It might need to be labeled as a special occasion dish. Just remember, it's your kitchen and you can do whatever you feel like, whenever you feel like it. You are the boss. If you don't feel like cooking, throw a wobbly and demand to be taken out.

2/3 cup of canned tamarind nectar
2/3 cup of canned mango nectar
2 very finely chopped shallots
1 tsp well aged balsamic vinegar
2 ozs non fat cream cheese softened
1/3 cup finely grated Parmesan
2 tsp fresh ginger paste (sold in small jars, usually next to the garlic)
1 tsp of red pepper flakes
1 tbsp fresh lemon juice
1 tbsp non fat sour cream
6 ozs crabmeat finely shredded
2 tbsp olive oil
1/2 tsp crushed garlic
8 really big jumbo shrimp in the shell but split down the back and de-veined
2 cups chicken stock
1/2 cup Basmati rice
6 fat asparagus spears
Fresh cracked black pepper
2 tbsp finely chopped cilantro

Put tamarind juice, mango juice, one of the chopped shallots and the balsamic in a small saucepan and simmer over medium heat until the liquid is thickened and reduced by about half. Take off the heat and set aside to cool. When cool, put in a blender and whiz until smooth. You can omit the blending part if you have better things to do. It will taste pretty much the same, but won't be quite as pretty with the bits of shallot visible to the naked eye. Sauce can be made in advance and kept covered and refrigerated until needed. Reheat prior to serving, and put into a small gravy boat or jug so it will pour it easily.

In a bowl combine the cream cheese, Parmesan cheese, the other chopped shallot, 1 tsp of the ginger paste, the red pepper flakes the lemon juice, sour cream and the crab meat and mix well. Mix the 2 tbsp olive oil with the crushed garlic and toss the shrimp in it. Now, with a spoon, fill each of the split shrimp with some of the crab mixture, pressing into place and mounding up as necessary. Place the shrimp, crabby side up, on a baking sheet and refrigerate until ready to broil

At this point get rice and asparagus ready. Heat the chicken stock in a small saucepan until boiling. Put in the rice and simmer until it is tender to the bite. Then strain, set aside and keep warm in the saucepan with a lid on it. Next, cheat, and cook asparagus in the microwave, it's really only for decoration anyway. Not worth making another pan or steamer dirty. Just clean it, trim it and put it on a plate, add 2 tbsp of water and cover with plastic wrap and cook on high heat for 2 minutes. Check for doneness by piercing with a sharp knife.

Pre-heat the broiler and retrieve the shrimp from the fridge. Broil them close to the broiler for about 2 minutes, then move them down to the middle shelf of the oven for about 8 minutes, and keep a careful eye on them. They should be delicately browned, but don't over cook them or they will be dry. Turn off the broiler and keep them in the warm oven while you set the plates up for serving.

To serve, press rice into a small ramekin and then invert onto plate, just sexily off center. It's also perfectly fine to dollop the rice on the plate with a spoon if you're in a more free form sort of mood. Cozy the shrimps up against the rice, and drizzle tamarind sauce over and around. Scatter an asparagus spear here and there, sprinkle with cilantro and it's done. Serve any extra sauce on the side.

Pan Seared Scallops with Arugula Couscous & Carrot Vinaigrette
For 2 (on a diet night)

I know, curry powder and carrot vinaigrette sounds a bit weird, but go wild......give it a chance, you might like it AND improve your night vision.

1/4 cup carrot juice (or any carrot/juice blend you fancy)
1/2 tsp Dijon mustard
1 tbsp sherry vinegar
1/2 tsp crushed garlic
4 tbsp olive oil
2 packed cups of baby arugula (or spinach if you prefer) washed and dried
12 grape tomatoes
12 large sea scallops (if you can get them with the orange feet still on even better)
1 cup water
2/3 cup whole wheat couscous
1 large shallot finely chopped
1/4 cup golden raisins
1 tsp curry powder
Salt and pepper for seasoning

First make the vinaigrette. In a screw top glass jar, put the carrot/fruit juice, mustard, sherry vinegar, garlic and 2 tbsp of the olive oil, then shake it until blended. Season with salt and pepper to taste. Pick a serving platter and arrange the arugula on it. Slice the grape tomatoes in half lengthways and scatter around the edge of the greens and pop the whole platter into the fridge to keep cold.

Now wash the scallops and pat them dry. Give them a good grind of black pepper on both sides. Heat the remaining 2 tbsp olive oil in a large non-stick sauté pan and set the oven to 325 degrees. When the oil is really hot put the scallops in and cook them for just a minute on each side. Don't over cook them or they will turn into bullets, and don't overcrowd them or the liquid they put out will stop them from browning. Better to cook them in very small batches to get them golden on the outside, and just barely cooked through. When done, pop them into the oven to stay warm.

While the scallops are all in the oven, bring the water to a boil, then take it off the heat and dump in the couscous the shallot, the golden raisins and the curry powder. Give it a stir, then cover with the lid and set aside for two minutes. Fluff with a fork to loosen it up before serving.

To finish up, drizzle half of the vinaigrette over the arugula and tomatoes, then spoon the fluffed couscous over the top. Now arrange the scallops on top and drizzle with the remainder of the vinaigrette. A little more fresh ground black pepper and you're ready to go. Serve with a few lightly steamed green beans or some sautéed zucchini slices if you wish.

Scallops & Shrimp with Rosemary & Polenta

For 2

This is my version of a dish I had at a very lovely hotel, overlooking the lake in Coeur D'Alene, Idaho. I think it was about 1996 and Felix and I had run away from home for Thanksgiving that year. Apparently, we were not in the mood for turkey.

You can make fresh polenta for this dish if you've lost your mind, or have no life. Just cook according to the package instructions and stir in some finely chopped fresh rosemary and some grated Parmesan cheese at the end. If you don't have time for this kind of nonsense, use the ready made logs of polenta. Easy…. and if you dress it up a bit…….quite palatable for a weeknight.

        1 roll of pre-made rosemary polenta
        8 tbsp extra virgin olive oil
        2 tbsp finely grated Parmesan
        1 shallot peeled and very finely chopped
        4 white mushrooms very finely chopped
        1 small tomato diced
        1/3 cup garbanzo beans
        2 very thin slices of prosciutto finely chopped
        1 tbsp finely chopped fresh rosemary
        Fresh cracked black pepper
        1/4 cup Madeira
        1/4 cup non fat sour cream
        6 jumbo shrimp peeled and de-veined
        6 large sea scallops washed and squeezed dry with paper towels.
        Extra sprigs of rosemary for garnish

Heat the oven to 375 degrees. Take the polenta roll and slice 4 half inch thick rounds from it. Heat 2 tbsp of the olive oil in a non-stick sauté pan and make sure it gets nice and hot before you do anything rash. Sauté the polenta rounds until they are nice and golden and crispy on both sides, then pop into a baking/serving dish. Sprinkle with the Parmesan and pop into the oven to bake for about 20 minutes.

While the polenta is baking, add 2 more tbsps olive oil to your sauté pan and get it nice and hot again. Sauté the shrimp, until they are barely cooked through, and set aside. Now add 2 more tbsps olive oil to the pan and sauté the scallops also until just barely cooked through and set aside with the shrimp. Don't overcrowd the pan or they will not brown. Wipe out the pan with paper towels and add the last 2 tbsp olive oil. Put in the shallots, mushroom, tomatoes, garbanzos and prosciutto and sauté for a couple of minutes. Add the rosemary and a few grindings of black pepper. Stir in the Madeira and the sour cream and turn heat down so it comes to a gentle simmer then add the shrimp and scallops back into the pan. Stir it all around so the seafood is warmed through and all nice and saucy.

To put it all together, slide two golden polenta rounds onto each plate and spoon the shrimp/scallop mixture over and around these. Garnish with a fresh rosemary sprig and cracked black pepper.

Miso Slathered King Salmon

For 2

This marinade is equally good on salmon, chicken, pork.......just about anything except chocolate really.....and don't think I haven't tried it.

  2 pieces of thick king salmon fillet (or any thick firm fish you fancy)
  2 tbsp flour
  1 heaped tbsp white or yellow miso paste
  1 tbsp honey
  1 tbsp mirin (Japanese cooking wine) (substitute white wine if you have no Mirin)
  1 tsp hot red pepper flakes
  2 tbsp olive oil

Pre-heat the oven to 375 degrees. Wash and pat dry your fish, and remove the skin if there is any. Rub the flour over both sides of the fish. In a shallow bowl mix together the miso, honey, mirin and pepper flakes, it should be a nice smooth paste, thick enough to cling to the fish and not run off. Now slather the mixture all over the fish, dip it right in the bowl if you need to.

Heat the oil in a non-stick skillet over medium high heat until nice and hot. Don't be tempted to put the fish in too early, have a little patience......pour yourself a glass of wine and compose yourself for goodness sake. When the pan is hot, pop the fish in and sear on one side for 2 minutes. Turn the fish over and sear the other side for 2 minutes. The miso paste should stick to the fish and turn a lovely golden color. After searing both sides, pop the fish into the oven and finish by roasting it for about 5 minutes. Test the fish by gently pulling the flakes apart and checking the center for doneness.

Salmon with Citrus Balsamic Reduction
For 2

This sauce is so good, even fish haters will eat this. If they don't like this, don't invite them back, because they're obviously deranged.

> 1/2 cup balsamic vinegar
> 1/2 cup dry white wine
> 2 tbsp fresh orange juice
> 2 tbsp fresh lemon juice
> 2 tbsp honey
> 2 tbsp olive oil
> 2 pieces thick salmon fillet skinned and patted dry
> 1 tbsp olive oil
> Fresh cracked black pepper

Pre-heat the oven to 375 degrees. Put the vinegar, wine, orange juice, lemon juice and honey into a small saucepan and bring to a boil. Turn down to medium/low and reduce carefully for about 10 minutes. It should get thicker and a bit syrupy, but don't overdo it or you'll end up with glue. Take off the heat and keep warm. If you do go too far and get the glue, carefully add a little water to the mix, stir and re-warm.

Heat the oil in a non-stick skillet and get it good and hot. Season the skinned salmon pieces with salt and pepper, pop into the pan, and sauté for 2 to 3 minutes each side, until just golden. Slide onto a baking sheet lined with non-stick foil and into the oven until just cooked through. About 7 to 8 minutes.

Slide a salmon piece onto each plate and drizzle the sauce over and around it. A little Caesar salad and some wild rice to go with this would be perfect.

Parmesan Crusted Halibut
For 2

Just about foolproof fish. The only way to mess this up is to leave it in the oven too long. The cheese crust keeps the fish so moist it doesn't really need a sauce, but just in case, a little lemon caper aioli on the side never hurt anyone.

  1/4 cup non fat mayonnaise
  1/4 cup non fat sour cream
  1 clove garlic, peeled and crushed
  2 tsp grated lemon zest
  2 tbsp fresh lemon juice
  1 tbsp white wine vinegar
  3 tbsp capers
  Fresh cracked black pepper to taste
  1 cup flour seasoned with salt and black pepper
  1 egg lightly beaten
  1 cup finely grated Parmesan cheese
  2 tbsp olive oil
  2 individual portions thick halibut fillet skinned (or any firm, thick white fish, cod etc.)

To make the aioli, put first 6 ingredients in a bowl and mix till smooth. Stir in the capers and pepper, then cover and refrigerate to allow flavors to blend.

Pre-heat the oven to 375 degrees. Put the flour, egg and cheese into individual dishes for dunking the fish into. Rinse the halibut and dry on paper towels. Heat the olive oil in a non stick sauté pan. While the oil is heating, dip the fish into the seasoned flour, then into the egg wash, and lastly cover it in grated cheese. When the oil is nice and hot, pop the fish in and cook for 2 minutes on each side. The cheese should form a nice golden crust all over it.

To finish the fish off, pop it into the oven for 6 to 7 minutes, maybe a tad longer, depending on how thick your fish is. You can transfer it to a small gratin type dish to bake, or you can leave it in the sauté pan, just make sure it has a metal handle (no rubber or plastic, or it will melt like the wicked witch of the west). The fish should be firm and maybe just a tiny bit opaque in the center to be perfect. Take a little vegetable knife and make a tiny gap between the flakes to make sure it's done to your liking.

Good with slow roasted tomatoes and some green beans that have been tossed with some Maytag blue cheese.

Halibut Kebabs

For 2

Another happy accident. Had no fresh ginger, substituted dried...... it was good.

    3/4 lb thick halibut fillet
    1/2 cup lemon juice
    1/2 tsp turmeric
    1/2 tsp crushed garlic
    1/2 tsp powdered ginger
    12 cherry tomatoes

Rinse the fish, pat it dry, then skin it and cut it into approximately 2 inch chunks. In a large freezer baggie, mix the lemon juice, turmeric, garlic and ginger and then slip the fish into it, shake it around a bit and then put in the fridge to marinate for at least an hour, preferably two.

Soak 4 wooden skewers in cold water for 30 minutes. Thread the chunks of fish and the whole cherry tomatoes onto the skewers and pop back into the fridge until you're ready to grill them.

You can cook these on a grill or an outside BBQ or under the broiler for that matter. Pre-heat whatever it is you're going to use, and then line a baking sheet with non-stick foil. Place the kebabs on the lined sheet and onto the grill or under the broiler. Cook for about 6 - 8 minutes, turning once, halfway through cooking.

Halibut with Gnocchi Leeks & Peas

For 2 – 3 (depending on gender and/or bodyweight of diners)

More wonderful stuff to do with halibut, which is good for me because it's as easy to find here in Seattle as fake Gucci is on Ebay. If halibut is not plentiful where you are, sturgeon, cod or sea bass would work just as well. Felix nearly passed out with joy when I first served him this.......he told me I should write a cookbook. Ha!

4 tbsp olive oil
1 lb thick halibut fillet
Fresh cracked black pepper
5 tender young leeks (small and thin)
1 cup frozen peas
1/2 cup non fat low sodium chicken stock
1 cup whole wheat gnocchi (From the nearest Italian deli of course)
1 tsp dried dill
1/4 cup dry white wine
2 tbsp lemon juice
2 tbsp non fat sour cream
4 thick asparagus spears washed and snapped at the tender point.
1 large lemon quartered

Pre-heat oven to 375 degrees. Skin and rinse your halibut fillet, then pat it dry and cut it into the individual size portions you want. Grind some fresh black pepper over the portions of fish. Heat 2 tbsp of the oil in a non-stick sauté pan and when it's hot, and only when it's hot, put in the fish, peppered side down, and give it just 2 minutes. Pepper the other side of the fish while the first side is having its 2 minutes and then turn it over and give it 2 minutes more. Now transfer the fish to an oven proof dish and just set it aside for a minute. Don't worry that it's not cooked through at this point, that's what the preheated oven is for. If I finish my fish in the oven, I find I never (okay rarely) overcook it.

Wipe the sauté pan out with a couple sheets of paper towel and put in the remaining 2 tbsp of oil. While the oil is heating, cut the top third off the green end of the leeks and strip off the outside layer from the whole leek, now slice each of them in half lengthways and rinse again. This will get rid of all the grit and dirt they are notorious for hiding in their folds. When they're clean, chop them into 2 inch lengths. When the oil is hot, sauté the leeks for 2 minutes, then add the frozen peas and sauté 3 minute more. Now add the chicken stock and gnocchi and stir it (gently) all about. Now, turn the heat down to low and cook, covered, for 5 gentle minutes. At this point, put the fish in the oven for 6-8 minutes, or until just cooked through. (This will depend on the thickness of your fish. If in doubt, get it out and pry apart the flakes with a couple of forks or a knife, so you can see how the middle is doing. Whatever you do, don't over cook it.)

Okay, back to the veggies, next add the dill, white wine, lemon juice, sour cream, stir it all about, and cook for 5 gentle minutes more. After 5 minutes, take off the heat, but leave the lid on, and set aside to just stay warm. While the fish and veggies are finishing up, put the asparagus in a microwaveable dish with a couple tablespoons of water and a good squeeze of lemon juice. Cover with clingwrap and microwave on high for 2 minutes. After 2 minutes, test it for tenderness by piercing with a sharp knife and when done, drain the liquid off and set aside.

When the fish is done to your liking, take wide, shallow soup bowls, and spoon some of the gnocchi/vegetable mixture into the bottom of each. Place a perfectly cooked piece of halibut on top of the gnocchi and vegetables, and then drape some asparagus seductively over one end of the halibut. Dust with more fresh ground black pepper, squeeze a lemon quarter over each dish and serve.

Mediterranean Calamari Pasta
For 4

There's just something about currants and calamari, not sure what it is but it drives me nuts with joy every time I eat this. It's also very good the following day, eaten cold, believe it or not.....but maybe it's just me that craves calamari for breakfast.

3 tbsp olive oil
1 medium sweet onion finely chopped
1/4 cup currants
1/4 cup pine nuts
1/4 cup Italian parsley finely chopped
1 tsp hot pepper flakes
1 cup crushed San Marzano tomatoes with juice
1/2 cup roasted red peppers finely chopped
1/2 cup clam juice
1/2 cup dry white wine
1 1/2 lbs calamari tubes (tubes cleaned and cut into rings and tentacles left whole)
Whole wheat linguini (however much your four people want)
1/4 cup chopped scallions for garnish

In a non-stick sauté pan heat 2 tbsp of the olive oil, then add the onion, currants, pine nuts, parsley and pepper flakes and sauté until the onion is soft and golden, about 10 minutes. Add the crushed tomatoes, peppers, the clam juice and the wine, and bring to a boil. Slide in the calamari and then simmer gently until the calamari is tender, about 10 minutes. While the calamari is simmering, cook the linguini in plenty of boiling water, then drain and set aside. When the calamari is done to your liking, toss the cooked linguini into the sauce and then tip the whole shooting match into a deep pasta bowl to serve. Remember the chopped scallions for garnish.

Paella

For 4 - 6 (*Impossible to make a small paella*)

This is a good one for an Italian Christmas Eve because you can stuff as much seafood in it as you like and thus take care of the seven fishes thing. It may seem a little labor intensive at first glance, but actually, lots of preparation can be done ahead and then the final dish can be assembled in quite a short time. It can even be cooked outside on a barbecue for a really authentic touch. The dish needs a large paella pan or sauté pan. A proper paella pan is a good investment, because you can get a nice crust on the bottom of the paella without worrying about burning your good sauté pan (for once it is correct to burn the bottom) and also, paella should be served right out of the pan, and a real paella pan looks much better on the table than a regular old sauté pan with its handle sticking out all over the place.

6 – 8 tbsp olive oil
6 chicken drummies or thighs, skinned and defatted.
2 hot Italian turkey sausages
1 lb thick, white fish cut into large chunks (monkfish, halibut, cod, scallops)
1/2 lb squid cleaned and sliced into rings and tentacles
1/2 lb medium shrimp, peeled and de-veined
1 tbsp butter
3/4 cup dry white wine
12 Manilla clams (scrubbed)
1 large sweet onion peeled and chopped
3 large Roma tomatoes diced
3 large cloves garlic, peeled and mashed
1/4 cup chopped fresh parsley
2 tbsp paprika (preferably half smoked paprika and half hot paprika but any will do)
1/4 cup tomato puree
1 1/2 cups short grain rice (Arborio is best, short grain brown rice can be used too but
    will take MUCH longer to cook and may require more liquid.)
32 ozs non fat low salt chicken broth (warmed)
Pinch of saffron (add to the warmed chicken broth)
1 cup frozen peas
4 whole cooked artichoke hearts quartered (canned or frozen)
1 large red bell pepper roasted, peeled, deseeded and sliced into thin strips
Lemon wedges

Pre-heat the oven to 375 degrees. In the paella pan, heat 2 tbsp of the olive oil over medium high heat. When hot, pop in the chicken thighs and sauté until nice and brown all over. When they are all brown put them in a small baking dish, add a little of the chicken stock, then cover with foil and bake in the oven for about 45 minutes or until the meat is falling off the bone tender. You can roast the red pepper at the same time if you don't have some already roasted in your freezer. Meanwhile, stick the sausages into the pan, brown them all over too and then set them aside. When cool enough, slice the sausages into

1/2" thick slices. Add a little more olive oil to the pan and quickly brown the fish chunks and or scallops (they don't have to be cooked right through) then sauté the shrimp and then the squid. Set each pile of partially cooked seafood aside as you are done. You may need to wipe out the pan with paper towels and add more olive oil if the seafood gives off a lot of liquid, otherwise it won't brown. The squid doesn't need to brown actually, just give it a quick sauté and be done with it. Wipe out the pan, when you're done with the seafood, but don't wash it.

In a small saucepan, heat the butter and the white wine, season with black pepper and when this is bubbling, add the clams to it and cover with a lid. Simmer this until all the clams open, then take them off the heat, drain and set aside. All the meats and seafood can be refrigerated at this point until you're ready to put the dish together.

When you're ready for final assembly, add a little more olive oil to the paella pan, then sauté the chopped onion, tomatoes, garlic and parsley until just sweated out. Then add the paprikas and the puree and stir it all together.

Now add the rice and half of the warmed chicken broth with the saffron, and the peas and stir everything about. Let this cook, stirring occasionally, over medium heat, for a few minutes. Next tuck the artichokes, the meats and seafood (but not the clams) into the pan mixture and continue to cook gently. **Don't stir the paella after this point, because, as mentioned earlier, in this case a burnt bottom is politically correct.** Gradually add the rest of the hot stock, and keep tasting the rice until it is al dente. You may need to turn the pan frequently so that it all cooks evenly, if you're cooking over a barbeque or open fire you won't need to. When the rice is almost there, tuck the clams down into the rice and drape the red pepper strips over the top. When the dish is done, most of the liquid should be absorbed, the rice will be tender and the dish will be a deep rich red color. A sea of tender rice studded with all those delicious chunks of chicken, sausage and seafood.

Serve right from the paella pan with plenty of lemon wedges to squeeze over the top. A little fresh parsley wouldn't hurt either.

Prosciutto Wrapped Monkfish with Passionfruit Sauce
For 2

Had something along these lines in St. Barths once and have been having passionate dreams about it ever since. Well what do you expect at my age?

1 cup non fat low sodium chicken stock
1 cup water
1/2 cup wild rice (you can use regular couscous, Israeli couscous or orzo if that's what you have on hand)
2 portions of fresh monkfish all membranes removed, (very important)
4 very thin slices of prosciutto (or enough to wrap your two pieces of fish)
1 tbsp Dijon mustard
1 tbsp non fat plain yogurt
1 tbsp olive oil
1/2 cup passionfruit juice (or any fruit juice you like)
1/4 dry white wine
1/4 cup non fat sour cream
Salt and pepper to taste

Pre-heat the oven to 375 degrees. Bring the stock and water to a boil in a medium saucepan. Rinse and drain the wild rice, then add to the boiling water. Reduce the heat a little and simmer until the rice is just tender, then drain, return to the saucepan, put the lid on and keep warm.

Trimming the monkfish of all membranes is absolutely essential, it will be tough, grey and weird looking if you don't…..trust me. Mix the mustard and yogurt together and spread this on the slices of prosciutto. Wrap two slices of the slathered prosciutto around each portion of the fish. The mustard/yogurt will stick the prosciutto to the fish. Heat the oil in a large non-stick sauté pan until nice and hot. Pop in the wrapped fish and sauté just until the packages are nicely browned and the prosciutto is getting a little crispy around the edges. Just a couple of minutes on each side. Now pop the fish into a small baking dish and into the oven for about 10 minutes to finish off. To check for doneness, pry a little between the prosciutto wrap edges with the points of a couple of sharp knives and it should be easy to tell if the fish is done in the middle to your liking.

While the fish is baking, return the sauté pan to the heat and pour in the passionfruit juice and the wine. Scrape up any bits from the bottom, then stir in the sour cream and make sure it's all well combined. Reduce heat to a simmer and reduce the sauce until it is nice and creamy, about 5 minutes season with salt and pepper as necessary.

To serve, mound the rice onto two plates, put a piece of the wrapped monkfish on top of each and then pour the sauce over and around. Garnish with more fresh cracked black pepper and maybe a little greenery for show.

Oven Baked Seafood Boil
For 4

Like a good Paella, this can also be cooked outside on a barbeque, and you can pretend you're on a beach in the Hamptons and not on the balcony of an apartment in Podunk, WA. You can add or substitute any kind of seafood you want, crab, chunks of firm fish, mussels etc. Everything works. There is a lot of hands on eating involved here, so once again, bibs and lots of paper napkins are good ideas.

16 manilla clams (or any decent sized clams).
2 tbsp cornmeal
4 hot Italian chicken or turkey sausages
8 small waxy potatoes (Yukon Golds or Yellow Finns)
8 jumbo shrimp de-veined
8 cocktail crab claws (or any bits of crab still in shell that you have taken a fancy to)
1 large sweet onion peeled and sliced
4 ears of fresh sweetcorn cut or broken into thirds
2 tsp hot red pepper flakes
1/2 cup fresh Italian parsley finely chopped
Fresh cracked black pepper
1 bottle blonde ale (light beer, lager etc.)

Scrub the clams, remove any beards, toss them into a bowl and cover with water. Add the 2 tbsp cornmeal and let them sit on the kitchen counter for an hour or two. Then drain, rinse and set aside. I've heard this cleans them out. Whether true or not, I have no clue, but I do it nonetheless.

Pre-heat the oven to 375 degrees. Cook the sausages, in the microwave, or the oven or however you like, then cut into 1/2" thick slices. Boil the potatoes in enough water to just cover them, until just barely tender, then cut each one into four pieces and set aside. Line a large deep baking dish with non-stick foil leaving an inch or two of foil overhanging the sides. Put the potatoes, onions, clams, shrimp, crab, sweetcorn and cooked sausages into the pan, sprinkle with the hot pepper flakes, the parsley and then some black pepper. Finally, pour over the beer, put more foil over the top of the whole thing and crimp the edges together to form a nice tight package. Pop into the hot oven for an hour and then take the top piece of foil off and serve straight from the dish. Hot crusty bread to mop up the juice.......fattening, but every now and then, there comes a time when a girl has to eat, what a girl has to eat.

Meat & Poultry...

Mum

I love my mum. She's short and sweet and just a lovely person through and through. She's also the only person I know who can bounce off an 11 or 12 hour transatlantic flight (cattle car mind you, not first class) and say everything was "lovely".....and she means the food too. And maybe the fact that she likes airline food is a bit of a clue, because as sweet as she is, she's not always been the greatest in the kitchen by any stretch. We had plenty to eat of course, but the menu was probably about as balanced as Britney Spears. To her credit, (my Mum's not Britney's) I did manage to grow up without scurvy, rickets or mange, but sometimes I wonder how. Just kidding Mum. She'll probably cut me out of her will for that one.

Like 99% of women, Mum is always trying to shed a few pounds and has tried pretty much every diet out there. Most recently it's been the South Beach Diet, and that has really sparked a lot of interesting culinary queries from her. **"Hello darling it's only me.....what's couscous?" "Antonia....it's Mum, what on earth is spaghetti squash?" "Me again, can you freeze pesto?"** She's a riot she really is, but at least she knows what pesto is.......I think.

Before South Beach however, there was Weightwatchers and this led to the infamous Lemon Chicken. Felix and I had been summoned for dinner one summer evening, and had been forewarned that we were to get Lemon Chicken as the plat du jour. I called Mums during the afternoon and asked if I could bring anything.....wine, flowers, extra lemons perhaps? **"Oh no dear"** she replied, **"There's no lemon in it".**

After I regained the power of speech, I begged her to tell me how one can possibly make Lemon Chicken with no lemon in it. I just had to know! Turned out it was made with lemonade powder and various other fake lemon products, but not a molecule of actual lemon. Shame on you Weightwatchers, taking advantage of little old English ladies. Despite knowing what was in it, we still showed up and duly tried to eat the stuff, but it was so, shall we say, unusual, that it made your eyes water. We didn't get through much of it I'm afraid, which meant my poor ol' stepdad probably had to pucker up and eat the leftovers for lunch the next day. Poor love. Mum's awfully strict about leftovers.

So, needless to say, I'm not going to offer my Mum's recipe for Lemon Chicken, but I do have a favorite of my own that is simplicity itself...... and full of lemons.

Lemon Chicken

For 4

A very old and very dear friend taught me this upside down trick years ago, and it really makes a difference. If you are not stunned and amazed at how tender and completely infused with lemon flavor this chicken is, I will eat my Charles David cork wedges. Weight Watchers......be afraid.

1 roasting chicken
2 small lemons (and a couple of wooden toothpicks)
Small bunch of fresh oregano
2 whole cloves garlic peeled and smashed once
Olive oil
Salt and pepper

Yes that's it. Pre-heat the oven to 375 degrees. Wash and pat the chicken dry with paper towels. Season inside and out with salt and pepper. Roll the lemons on a cutting board with your hand to free up the juices inside and then prick them all over with a toothpick so that all the lovely lemon juice will pour out. Stuff the lemons, the oregano and the garlic into the cavity of the chicken and then close the flaps with the toothpicks to keep all the goodies inside. Rub the chicken all over with olive oil, put it breast side down into a roasting pan and pop into the pre-heated oven. After 40 minutes, carefully turn the chicken over and continue roasting until done. Should be about another 40 minutes. Pierce the thickest part of a thigh with a skewer and the juices will run clear when the bird is done. If it is getting too browned, put some foil loosely over the top to finish cooking. When you get it out of the oven, let it sit and rest for 5 minutes, loosely covered with foil. Incredible stuff. Makes good sandwiches when cold too.

Chicken Parmesan
For 4

This is fast, completely idiot-proof and wonderful every time. Quick enough for a weekday night, fancy enough for a dinner party.

The other great thing about this dish is you can assemble it ahead of time, to the point where it's ready to pop into the oven, and then all you have to do is bake it for 10 minutes or so before you want to serve it. Once again leaving you beautifully free for mingling with your guests...... or watching the Nightly News with Brian Williams. Just love him, don't you?

4 boneless skinless chicken breasts
1/2 cup seasoned flour
1 lightly beaten egg
1 cup panko breadcrumbs
2 tbsp olive oil
4 roasted red bell pepper slices (use store bought if you haven't roasted your own)
2 tbsp fresh basil chopped
1 ball of fresh Mozzarella sliced
1 1/2 cups fresh tomato sauce
2 tbsp finely grated Parmesan cheese

First of all pre-heat the oven to 400 degrees. Lay a chicken breast between two sheets of plastic wrap and beat on it with a rolling pin or a heavy pot or a meat tenderizer, it doesn't matter what as long as you flatten it evenly to about 1/4 to 1/2 inch thick all over. Repeat with the other breasts and season both sides with salt and pepper.

Dip the chicken breasts in the flour, then in the egg and then in the breadcrumbs. Set the breaded chicken aside. If you want to cut down the calories a bit more you can dispense with the flour, egg and breadcrumbs and just sauté the seasoned, but naked chicken. It's still very good.

Heat the oil in a non stick sauté pan. When you're sure it's nice and hot, pop the chicken in and just sear for a minute or so on each side. The chicken should be nice and golden brown, but it will not be cooked through. Remove the chicken from the pan and place in a baking dish. Put a slice of roasted red pepper on each chicken breast then scatter the basil over the pepper. Arrange the sliced Mozzarella over the basil and drizzle tomato sauce over each breast. Last of all, sprinkle the Parmesan over all. You can make to this point ahead of time then just cover until you are ready to bake. It will take just 10 to 15 minutes, to reach bubbling perfection.

Skinny Chicken Enchiladas
For 2

I know enchilada is a very scary word to those of us with carb sensitive thighs, but these skinny little darlings are flabuless. Sounds a lot for two I know, but I can eat two of these, and for Felix there really is no limit.

> 1 cup non fat low sodium chicken stock
> 1 cup water
> 2 tsp red pepper flakes
> Fresh ground black pepper
> 2 boneless skinless chicken breasts
> 1/2 large sweet onion chopped
> 1/4 cup hot salsa
> 1/4 cup non fat cream cheese
> 1/4 cup non fat sour cream
> 1 cup grated Cheddar cheese (I have used non fat or low fat in the past too, and it's really
>   not that bad at all)
> 1/2 cup roasted red peppers peeled, seeded and roughly chopped
> 1 cup San Marzano tomatoes with some juice, roughly chopped
> 5-6 whole wheat tortillas (depends on how generously you want to stuff them)

Heat the chicken stock and 1 cup of water in a large saucepan to a simmer, add 1 tsp red pepper flakes and a few grinds of black pepper. When the water is at a gentle simmer slide the chicken breasts in and poach VERY gently for 20 minutes. Don't boil or the chicken will be tough. Remove chicken and set aside to cool. When nice and cool, shred with your fingers.

In a bowl combine the chopped onion, salsa, cream cheese, sour cream and 1/3 cup of the cheddar cheese and then add the shredded chicken and mix it all about until well combined.

Put the roasted red peppers and the tomatoes in a blender and add the remaining red pepper flakes and some fresh ground black pepper and whiz for a minute or so.

Pre-heat the oven to 375 degrees and select a non stick baking pan which will hold six enchiladas. Oil the bottom of the pan or spread a little of the red pepper/tomato sauce over the bottom. Take a tortilla and put some of the chicken mixture in the center and roll up. Put in the baking pan, seam side down, and repeat with the other tortillas until pan is full. Pour the red pepper/tomato sauce all over the rolled up enchiladas then cover with foil and bake for 20 minutes. Remove from oven, take off the foil and sprinkle the remaining 2/3 cup of cheddar cheese over the top. Now bake for another 5 minutes and devour.

Chicken Brie & Mango Chutney in Phyllo
For 2

Cute, quick, little packets of poultry. In my experience, if you want to impress people with food......
wrap it in something......and phyllo (or filo) is an excellent choice of wrapping material. Thankfully, as
in all my favorite recipes, little time, and even less skill, is required to pull off this illusion of magnificence
in the kitchen. All you need is a package of defrosted phyllo dough, and some experience with Christmas
presents.

Phyllo is wonderful stuff by the way. It's low cal because it's mostly made of fresh air I think, and yet you
still get that naughty, post-pastry feeling after eating it.

    2 boneless, skinless chicken breasts
    3 ozs Brie cheese (you can remove the rind if you like, we eat the whole thing)
    4 tbsp mango chutney (Major Grey's is pretty good)
    8 sheets thawed phyllo dough (keep covered with damp towel after you remove from
        package)
    1/4 cup olive oil
    Fresh cracked black pepper

Pre-heat the oven to 400 degrees. Make a lengthways slit in the fattest side of the chicken breast and form
a pocket in which to put the cheese and chutney. Slide half of the brie and half of the chutney into each
chicken breast pocket and pull the edges closed. Season with fresh cracked black pepper.

Lay one sheet of phyllo dough on your work surface and lightly brush with olive oil. Keep the other
sheets covered with a damp cloth or they will dry up and crack on you. You don't have to be too meticu-
lous with the oil coverage, just slap it on. Lay another sheet of phyllo dough on top and brush that with
oil too. Repeat with two more layers of phyllo dough, then place the stuffed chicken breast in one corner
of the phyllo sheets and wrap it up like a Christmas present. Brush the tops of the packages with a little
olive oil and place them on a baking sheet. Into the oven for 35 minutes and they're ready to eat. Check
on them after 20 minutes and if the phyllo is browning too much, just drape a sheet of foil over the top
for the remainder of the cooking time.

Moussaka

For 4

Hard not to love this dish; wine, meat, garlic, tomatoes, cheese.....so far couldn't be better. Easy to throw together, one dish to wash, and great cold for breakfast. (I suppose you've gathered by now that I'm not a cereal fan.)

    1 large eggplant
    6 tbsps olive oil
    1 medium sweet onion, finely chopped
    1/2 lb lean ground lamb
    1/2 lb lean ground beef
    1/4 lb lean ground veal (you can use all lamb or all beef if you prefer)
    14 oz can of San Marzano tomatoes with juice (chop the tomatoes)
    3 tbsp of tomato puree
    2 tsps dried oregano
    1 tsp crushed garlic
    1/4 cup red wine
    1 cup crumbled Feta cheese
    1 1/2 cups plain non fat yogurt
    1 large egg lightly beaten (or 1/4 cup of eggbeaters)

Pre-heat the oven to 375 degrees. Trim the end off the eggplant and slice it lengthwise into thin slices about 1/4 to 1/2 inch thick. Line a baking sheet with non-stick foil and pop the eggplant on it in a single layer. Brush all the slices with some of the oil and pop into the oven. Bake for about 10 - 12 minutes and then turn the slices over, brush again with oil and bake for another 10 - 12 minutes. The eggplant should be soft and somewhat browned.

While the eggplant is cooking, heat the remainder of the olive oil in a large, non-stick sauté pan over medium high heat. When the oil is hot, pop in the onion and sauté until golden. Add the ground meats and continue to cook, breaking up the lumps of meat with a wooden spoon. When all the meat is browned, pour off any excess fat. If you have used very lean meats, you might not have to do this bit at all. Now add the tomatoes and their juice, the tomato puree, oregano, garlic and red wine. Stir all about and let it simmer for a few minutes. It needs to be quite thick, no excess liquid, so keep cooking until the sauce is nice and tight and then take off the heat.

Take a 12" square baking dish (or something that's as close as makes no never mind) and place a layer of eggplant over the bottom. Now spoon one third of the meat sauce over the top. Divide the Feta cheese into two piles. Then sprinkle a little (about 1/3) of one of the piles of cheese over the meat sauce. Add another layer of eggplant, another layer of meat and a little more Feta. Then repeat. (This will use only one of the piles of Feta.) Cover the dish with foil and pop into the 375 degree oven for about an hour.

While the eggplant/meat thingy is baking away, make the topping. Into a small bowl put the yogurt, the remaining pile of finely crumbled Feta cheese and the egg and beat together well. After baking for an hour, take the meat thingy out of the oven, pour the topping over and spread it all around to cover the meat base. Increase the oven heat to 400 degrees and pop the moussaka back in for about 20 minutes. You can brown it under the broiler to get it a bit more golden if you like.

Now you have everything you need for a mini Greek vacation. Turn the heat up and put on your shorts. Serve some hummus for an appetizer, make a little Greek salad with lots of olive oil, Feta cheese, garlic, cucumber, tomatoes and olives, to go with the Moussaka and you can just about smell the breeze coming off the Aegean.

Hearty Meat Ragu with Pappardelle Noodles
For 6 (or more depending on how much sauce you like on your noodles)

This is my interpretation of a really thick, hearty Italian meat ragu. Felix is always bemoaning the fact that I don't put in a pig's tail or a pig's trotter for flavor, like his Grandma used to, but I can't, I just can't, because I simply cannot ignore that I know where they've been, and more likely than not, what the previous owner did with them too. Anyway, this is a multi-talented sauce as it can also be incorporated into Lasagne, baked with gnocchi or eaten right out of the pot. It freezes well too so I often make double batches.

    1/2 lb ground veal
    1/2 lb ground pork
    1/2 lb lean ground beef
    2 sweet Italian sausages skinned (you can use turkey to keep the fat down if you like)
    2 tbsp olive oil
    1 medium sweet onion very finely chopped
    2 stalks celery very finely chopped
    1 28 oz can crushed tomatoes
    2 cloves garlic crushed
    2 bay leaves
    1 tbsp dried oregano or marjoram
    2 ozs finely chopped prosciutto
    1/4 cup tomato paste (no salt)
    1 cup non fat low sodium chicken stock
    1 cup red wine
    Pappardelle noodles (or tagliatelle) for 6

Get a nice big sauté pan or shallow soup pot and set it over medium high heat. Pop in the ground meats and sauté gently, stirring around to break it up and brown it all over. It will start to give off some fat and liquid. Let this accumulate and then pour the excess fat and liquid off into a bowl. Break up the sausage and add to the ground meats. Stir this all around to mix it up and cook for about 10 minutes. You can strain off more fat and liquid after this time if you like, or you can be bad and leave it in for extra flavor. (You'll be glad you poured it off when you see it set in the bowl.......all that fat would be clogging your arteries or worse still, dimpling up your thighs.) Pour the defatted meats into a bowl and set aside.

Now add the olive oil to the sauté pan and get it nice and hot. Add the chopped onion and celery and sauté for 5 to 6 minutes until just starting to brown. Add the meats back to the pan and all the rest of the ingredients (except the pasta) and stir around. Turn the heat to low, put a lid on it and allow it to sit on the back burner for at least 2 hours. (The longer the better really and if you can then let it sit overnight in the fridge and re-heat it the next day, it's pure magic.) Anyway, stir it frequently and after two hours or so, it should be thick and red. If the sauce gets too thick, add more chicken stock, wine or water, if it's too thin, take the lid off and cook a while longer.

Now all you have left to do is cook the noodles in plenty of boiling water with a little salt and olive oil added. When they are al dente, drain them, toss them with as much of the sauce as suits you and tip into a large pasta bowl. Grate plenty of Parmesan cheese over the top, grab a nice bottle of Chianti and dig in. Go on.....you can tuck your napkin under your chin if you like, nobody needs to know.

Mediterranean Lamb Kebabs with Pitas & Tzatziki
For 2 (big eaters)

Garlic, garlic and more garlic, so share it with someone you love.

For the Marinade
3/4 cup of non fat yogurt
Zest and juice of 1 medium lemon
1 tbsp dried oregano
1 very large garlic clove peeled and crushed (or 2 small)
1 tsp ground cumin

Also
3/4 lb of lamb leg meat cut into large cubes (about 2" square)
3 or 4 Greek style pita breads

For the Tzatziki
1 cup non fat yogurt
4 inches English cucumber coarsely grated, skin and all
2 cloves garlic peeled and crushed
1/4 cup fresh lemon juice
Fresh cracked black pepper

In a bowl mix all the marinade ingredients and stir well. Put the lamb in and mix it around to cover it all. Cover the bowl and let the lamb marinate. The longer the better really, overnight is best, but a minimum of 3 hours.

If using wooden skewers soak them in water for a couple of hours before threading the meat onto them. If using metal skewers you don't have to worry.

After the lamb has marinated long enough, thread the cubes onto your skewers loosely, don't pack them too tightly or they won't cook evenly. Now grill them on a nice hot, oiled grill for about 3 or 4 minutes per side, depending on how pink you like your lamb, and how hot your grill is. Heck, give them to your man thing and tell him to cook them, you've done all the work so far!

While the lamb is grilling, mix all the tzatziki ingredients together in a small bowl and refrigerate. Just before the lamb is ready, put your pita breads on the grill to warm through and get those lovely grill marks on the outside. Grab a skewer and pull the lamb off, pile onto the warm pita, drench with garlicky tzatziki, fold up and tuck in.

Roasted red peppers go nicely in these too if you want another layer of flavor. I have also been known to put a couple spoonfuls of tabouleh in with the lamb before smothering it in Tzatziki. Grilled onions, any kind of Greek salad, you get the idea…...

Osso Bucco My Way
For 2

If you have an aversion to eating veal you can make this with lamb shanks instead. I found this out a long time ago when I was planning to serve Osso Bucco at a dinner party. I lived in the wilderness at the time, with nary a real butcher to be found, so veal shanks were a pretty rare commodity. Not to be deterred, I placed a special order, with the meat department of my local grocery store. On Saturday morning, I arrived to pick up my order, only to be met with "What veal shanks?" After I calmed down and let the butcher go, I found 6 nice lamb shanks and trotted off home with those. The dish came out very nicely, and since then, I have often made this recipe with lamb by choice.

Osso Bucco is traditionally served with a thick, tomato based sauce. Now while this is very good, we seem to prefer it my way. I still like to serve it with a little side of risotto though, just like the traditional version.

4 tbsp olive oil
2 nice big veal shanks (or 4 little ones)
1/4 cup of well seasoned flour
1 large clove garlic minced
1 medium onion sliced
1 carrot sliced into 1/4 inch thick discs
1 stick celery chopped into 1/4 inch thick slices
1 15 oz can ceci beans (aka chickpeas or garbanzos)
Zest and juice of 1 lemon
2 tbsp dried oregano
1/4 cup of capers drained
2 cups non fat low sodium chicken stock
Salt and fresh cracked pepper

Pre-heat the oven to 350 degrees. Heat 2 tbsp of the olive oil in a sauté pan until nice and hot. While this is heating, dredge the shanks in the seasoned flour. Now brown the shanks on all sides in the hot sauté pan. When they are suitably golden and to your liking, remove from pan and set aside. In the same sauté pan add the rest of the olive oil, then put in the garlic, onion, carrots and celery, and sauté for 4 to 5 minutes. When the vegetables are softened and the onions slightly browned, pour them all into a deep baking dish. Drain and rinse the chickpeas and add them to the baking dish. Now pop the browned shanks on top of the beans and vegetables, and sprinkle everything with the zest, lemon juice, oregano and capers. Pour the chicken stock around the shanks and cover tightly with either a lid, or foil. Pop into the oven for at least 1 1/2 hours. Check it about half way through and make sure all the stock has not evaporated. If the liquid level is low, add a little more stock or water. The meat should be falling off the bone tender. If not, bake it some more, adding more stock as necessary until it complies with your wishes.

Saltimbocca
For 4

This is my favorite dinner party dish because it can be pre-assembled, requires very little skill and tastes pretty fabulous. You can make it with small, boneless, skinless chicken breasts if you have an aversion to eating baby cows.

4 veal scaloppini (you may need two or more apiece if the pieces are small)
1/2 cup flour
Fresh ground black pepper and salt
6 – 8 tbsp olive oil
4 slices very thinly sliced prosciutto (about same size as scaloppini if possible)
8 fresh sage leaves (4 whole, and 4 finely chopped)
4 wafer thin slices of Parmesan cheese (about same size as scaloppini if possible)
1 tbsp butter
1/2 cup dry white wine
1 tbsp fresh lemon juice
1/4 cup non fat sour cream

Take the veal slices and pound each one between two pieces of cling wrap until nice and thin. I use a rolling pin which is tapered at both ends. This pounding, as well as being good for the soul, also makes the veal very tender. Season the flour with salt and pepper and then dredge the meat in it. Heat 2 tbsp of the oil in a large non-stick sauté pan over medium high heat and while you're at it, line a cookie sheet with non-stick foil. Let the pan get good and hot and then flash fry the flour dredged meat until just lightly browned on both sides. You may need to add more olive oil to the pan between each batch. Don't over cook it, or it will be tough. All you want to do at this point is add that little bit of brown color. When each slice is lightly browned to your liking, transfer to the cookie sheet. Take off the heat, but don't wash the sauté pan yet.

Now put a piece of the prosciutto on top of each slice of meat, then a whole sage leaf and then a slice of the Parmesan cheese. Cover the cookie sheet with more foil. You can leave the dish on hold at this point if you like, and finish it up just before you're ready to serve.

When ready to serve, heat the oven to 400 degrees. Add a tablespoon of olive oil and a tablespoon of butter to the sauté pan and heat to medium. Toss in the chopped sage and sauté for a few seconds, then add the wine and lemon juice and then stir in the sour cream. Scrape all the veal bits off the bottom and it will combine into a nice smooth sauce. Reduce it for a few seconds if the sauce is too thin, then take off the heat. When the oven is hot, pop in the meat on the covered cookie sheet and bake for 5 minutes. Pull it out of the oven, uncover and pour over the sauce from the sauté pan. Pop back into the oven for 2 more minutes, uncovered and then serve. Extra lemon wedges, black pepper and more sage, are nice extras.

Lamb Baked with Gnocchi

For 2 (very generous helpings)

This is the kind of dish I would serve if I owned a bistro. Not very good for the hips, but wonderful for the soul. I tend not to make my own gnocchi anymore, as I have a life, and I can get them from the nearest Italian deli. Most supermarkets have them in the pasta aisle nowadays too.

    2 tbsp olive oil
    3/4 lb of stewing lamb cut into 1" cubes
    1 tsp fennel seeds
    1/2 medium sweet onion peeled and chopped
    1 tbsp dried oregano
    1 large garlic clove peeled and crushed
    1/2 small fennel bulb trimmed and chopped
    1/2 small eggplant chopped into half inch cubes
    1/2 red bell pepper seeded and chopped
    1 1/2 cups chopped San Marzano tomatoes with their juice
    1/3 cup tomato paste
    1/2 cup dry red wine
    1/2 cup beef stock
    1 cup whole wheat gnocchi
    1/2 cup of fresh Mozzarella cheese cut into small chunks
    Salt and black pepper
    1/2 cup finely grated Parmesan cheese

In a large sauté pan, heat the olive oil over high heat. When hot, put in the lamb and sauté until evenly browned. You might want to do this in two batches, it will brown better that way. As the meat browns, set it aside in a bowl to catch any juices it releases. Once all the lamb is browned, put the fennel seed, onion, oregano, garlic, fennel bulb, eggplant and red pepper into the same pan and sauté for 4 to 5 minutes. Add the tomatoes, tomato paste, the red wine, the beef stock and the lamb and season with salt and pepper. Cover the stew with a lid and turn the heat down to very low. Let this simmer on the back burner until the lamb is meltingly tender, about 1 1/2 hours. You can't overcook this.

While the lamb is cooking, bring a large pot of salted water to a boil and add a splash of olive oil. When the water is boiling, slide in the gnocchi and cook them until they float to the surface. You might want to turn the heat down a bit, so they are at a gentle boil, not a violent one. When they all float, drain them and set them aside. You can toss them with a little olive oil if you like to stop them sticking to each other.

When the lamb and the gnocchi are both done, pre-heat the oven to 375 degrees. Gently fold the gnocchi and the Mozzarella into the lamb stew and then pour the mixture into a deep casserole dish. Cover this with foil and bake in the oven for 35 minutes. Uncover the dish, sprinkle with the Parmesan and return to the oven for five minutes.

Best Ever Ribs

For 5 (maybe 6 but I doubt it)

I have had marriage proposals after serving these, but looking back, I'm beginning to think they were probably the result of rib-induced delirium and not truly heart felt declarations of undying love. Whatever…..not one of them was my type anyway.

> 4 racks baby back ribs
> Water
> Your favorite barbeque sauce (Armadillo brand is my favorite, a hot/spicy but fruity one)
> 1/2 cup of red currant jelly (warmed in a small saucepan)

Pre-heat the oven to 325 degrees. Get a deep roasting dish or baking dish and put a wire rack inside. You might need two, depending on the size of your roasting equipment. Fill baking dish halfway with water and place the rib racks on top, convex side up. Cover tightly with foil and slide into the heated oven. Roast gently for 2 1/2 to 3 hours, check on the water level now and again to make sure they don't get dry. This is the secret to truly great ribs. You can do anything your little heart desires to them after this and they will still be fantastic.

After the requisite time, the ribs will be pale and the ends of the bones will be sticking out from the meat about half an inch to an inch or so. Let them cool and then slather them thickly with your barbeque sauce. Cover them up and pop them in the fridge to rest until you're ready to finish them off.

You can grill them on a barbeque or you can bake them in the oven. Either way, get the source of heat fired up. The oven should be at 375 degrees. I don't do barbeques, so I'd leave the state of the barbeque to the nearest man if I were you. Retrieve ribs from the fridge, cover them with foil and pop them into the oven. I give them a good 35 minutes covered and then I uncover them and roast them uncovered until they get nice and brown around the edges, about another 20 minutes. Now they have got a bit of a roast on them, brush them with the redcurrant jelly and return them to the oven for a final 10 minutes.

When they are done to your liking, pull them out of the oven and slide onto a cutting board. With a sharp knife, cut them into individual riblets. Serve them on a big white platter with plenty of napkins and stand back.

Perfect Pepper Steak
For 2

My dad is a purist when it comes to his meat........he likes to taste the meat, not a sauce. But occasionally, when he's feeling mellow, he will allow someone to cook him a pepper steak. I think he'd like this one.

    3 tbsp olive oil
    1 large clove very finely chopped garlic
    1 shallot peeled and very finely chopped
    1 tsp miso paste
    1 tsp soy sauce
    1 tsp Worcestershire sauce
    3 tbsp green peppercorns (Not the dried ones, the ones in liquid in jars)
    4 tbsp coarsely cracked black peppercorns
    1/4 cup Brandy
    1/4 cup beef stock
    1 tbsp butter
    2 very thick filet mignons at room temperature

Heat 1 tbsp of the olive oil in a large non-stick sauté pan. Sauté the garlic and shallots until just golden, add the miso paste, soy and Worcestershire sauces, the green peppercorns and 1 tsp of the cracked black pepper, then stir around and cook for a couple of minutes. Add the Brandy and the stock and bring back to a boil. Turn down the heat, and simmer this gently for 2 to 3 minutes, then add the butter and allow it to melt into the sauce. Take off the heat and set the sauce aside.

Heat the oven to 400 degrees. Rub the steaks with 1 tbsp of the remaining olive oil and then press both sides of the steaks into the rest of the cracked black pepper. Heat the last 1 tbsp olive oil in a sauté pan and sauté the steaks over high heat for 2 minutes per side. Pop into the hot oven to finish off for 5 minutes. You can grill the steaks over high heat if you prefer. Re-warm the pepper sauce.

To plate up, put the steak in the middle of a nice warm dinner plate and pour the pepper sauce over the top. That's it.......Dad doesn't like vegetables to get in the way of his meat either.

Vegetables Only...

We don't just eat fish and chips and bangers and mash; English people are excellent gardeners and we love our veggies too.

England

I have to admit, I'm cut to the quick when I hear people say that English food is bad. It's just a vicious rumor you know, and one that I have a sneaking feeling was started by the French. (No doubt in retaliation for the one we started about their aversion to soap.) It's nothing new though; the English and the French have been engaged in one petty squabble or another for many centuries, and we'll probably be hurling insults at each other over the English Channel for many more to come.

But never mind who started it, the worst Brit bashing I ever heard was on a British Airways flight from London to Houston. The plane was full of Texans returning home from vacation, and, of course, little old me. The Texans were not using inside voices, and as far as I could gather, their blood cheeseburger levels were disturbingly low. Apparently, not one of them had encountered anything even remotely edible for the last two weeks, and they'd lost at least 400 lbs between them. When the plane touched down there was a lot of cheering, stomping of feet, and even some dancing in the aisles. It certainly didn't look like they were weak from lack of food, so I kept my head down and tried not to look too English. Hey, they just might have been hungry enough and I hear we taste like pork.

My point though, is that there's good and bad food to be found everywhere, including England. I take that back, I forgot Sweden, where it's all bad. Just kidding, but cold herring, lox and all that snow sounds rather unappealing. Fine if you're a penguin, but personally, in a climate like that, I'm going to be in the Four Alarm Chili line.....but I digress. According Felix (who is very keen on eating) some of the best food he's ever had has been in England.....in good old English pubs. Felix loves pubs in general, because they all have beer, but there's one in particular, the mere mention of which sets him all of a quiver. The Black Dog.

Almost all English pubs have great names as well as great food. City pubs often seem to be dubbed in honor of various bits and pieces of royal anatomy. For example, Kings Heads and Queens Heads, pop up quite a bit, and this is probably because the British have chopped a lot of these off over the years, and we like to remember our beheaded. The country establishments go for names with more rural overtones, like the Pig and Whistle or the Ferret and Pitchfork. In these places you'll find lots of farmers, usually accompanied by sheepdogs (aka border collies) most of which also drink beer, and open their own bags of crisps. (You think I'm kidding don't you!) Otherwise, there are lots of White Horses, Black Horses and frequently Foxes and Hounds are involved.

There are Mermaids, and Dolphins, Bells, Boots, and Ploughs, and at least 10 million pubs called The Ship.

But anyway, back to The Black Dog. A good few years ago, Felix and I were on the road between London and Plymouth, which is in the county of Devon. Felix was driving, and I was trying hard to think of a way to make him stop. Let's just say, when the steering wheel is on the wrong side of the car, and he has to drive on the wrong side of the road as well, it's not pretty. And the roundabouts….don't even ask about the roundabouts. Peering though white knuckles, I saw several versions of the end of the world as I know it, and I must say I didn't fancy any of them. I tried offering gentle suggestions, interspersed with some blood curdling screams, but nothing seemed to help. Horns were blaring, fingers were being raised, and I was down to the quick on all 10 digits.

Felix was actually enjoying himself, but of course he's Italian, and thereby genetically engineered for dangerous driving. I however am not, and I knew I had to get him out from behind the wheel before I passed out and he had to drive the rest of the way to Devon, God forbid, unsupervised. Then I spotted the sign, "Good Food and Fine Ales….This way to The Black Dog". The sign was shaped like a finger and pointed enticingly off down a tiny lane to our left. A rural pub…..the perfect way to entice Felix from behind the wheel.

We started off down the lane, which immediately became even narrower, and grew 6 foot high hedges on both sides. The last thing I really remember was thinking, **"At least Felix doesn't have to choose which side of the road to drive on now"**, and then all hell broke loose. Those roundabouts had been nothing. Three foot wide lanes, along which the locals drove Land Rovers, herds of cattle, or large farm tractors at 70 mph, depending on their whim, where much worse. Twenty terror filled minutes later we pulled to a stop in the parking lot of the pub and I flung myself out of the car and headed for the pub……there had to be Chardonnay in there!

There was indeed, and after a couple glasses of it, and a truly splendid lunch, the terrors of the drive receded like my uncle Phil's hairline, and all was well with the world. So, the truth of the matter is, there IS wonderful food in England and English people CAN cook. If anyone doubts it, try the Leek Potato and Stilton Bake at the Black Dog…….it's on the A303……just remember to fasten your seatbelt.

Leek Potato & Stilton Bake
For 4

I've taken the liberty of adding a few shitake mushrooms to the Black Dog classic, and Felix seems to like it even better......in fact I think he would roll in it like a happy Labrador if not watched closely.

2 large baking potatoes peeled and cut into large chunks

2 tbsp olive oil

4 large leeks trimmed, split down the middle, thoroughly washed and chopped into 2" lengths

8 ozs shitake mushroom caps sliced.

1/4 cup of Madeira (or whatever Sherry type thing you may have lurking in your liquor cabinet)

3 tbsp butter

3 tbsp flour

2 cups milk

1/3 cup Stilton cheese crumbled (or any blue cheese you fancy)

1/3 cup white Cheddar cheese grated.

Pop the chunks of potatoes into boiling, lightly salted water, and then simmer until they are just tender/firm, but not falling apart. Drain and set aside. (If you are short on time, you can cook the potato chunks in a microwave.) Heat the olive oil in a large sauté pan and sauté the chopped leeks and the shitakes for about 5 minutes, then add the Madeira and a grind or two of fresh black pepper. Continue to cook until all liquid is absorbed or evaporated, about 5 more minutes. When the leeks and mushrooms are cooked, toss the potatoes into the sauté pan with them and set aside.

Pre-heat the oven to 375 degrees. In a saucepan heat the butter until melted, then take off the heat briefly and stir in the flour until you have a smooth paste. Put back on the heat and gradually pour in the milk, whisking constantly to prevent lumps forming. Keep the pan over medium heat and keep whisking until the sauce thickens. When it has thickened up sufficiently, add the crumbled Stilton, the grated Cheddar and stir well. Cook until cheese has melted into sauce and completely combined. Season to taste with salt and pepper, pour over your veggies and mushrooms and mix it all about. Now butter (or oil) an 8x8 gratin dish and pour the mixture in. Bake in the preheated oven for 45 minutes, or until nice and golden brown on top.

Eggplant Fritters with Tomato Basil Sauce
Makes 8

More eggplant, we love eggplant in Britaly, it's not fattening, unless you absolutely soak it in olive oil, and I've heard it's also good for keeping the cholesterol demons at bay.

    1 large eggplant
    Olive oil for brushing and sautéing
    1 cup stale bread torn into chunks and firmly packed
    3/4 cup milk
    1 cup finely grated Parmesan cheese
    1 tsp crushed garlic
    2 eggs (lightly beaten)
    1/4 cup chopped fresh parsley
    1/4 cup chopped fresh basil
    1/4 cup currants
    1/4 cup pine nuts
    1/2 cup panko breadcrumbs
    1 1/2 cups tomato basil sauce (see Britalian Kitchen)

First of all, preheat the oven to 375 degrees, then peel the eggplant and cut it into 4 quarters, lengthways. Brush generously with olive oil, pop into the oven and roast until very soft, about 20 minutes. Turn the eggplant pieces a couple of times during cooking and brush with more oil if they look a bit dry. When the eggplant is suitably cooked, remove from the oven and set aside to cool.

While eggplant is cooling take the stale bread and soak it in cold milk until it's soft, then squeeze all the excess moisture out of it and set the soaked bread aside. Once the eggplant is cool, coarsely chop it. Now drag out the food processor and toss in the eggplant, soaked bread, 1/2 cup of the Parmesan, garlic, 1 egg, parsley and basil. Process this lot for a minute until it's nicely blended, but not too smooth, some lumps are good, as long as they are not on one's thighs. Stir in the currants and pine nuts.

Now take a small handful of the eggplant mixture and form into a flattened disk, about the sized of a squashed golf ball. Press lightly into the remaining egg and then the panko breadcrumbs on both sides and set aside. Make all the fritters this way, and then heat a couple of tablespoons of olive oil in a non-stick sauté pan until nice and hot. Then turn heat to medium high and put in a first batch of 4 fritters, not too many at a time because you'll need room to turn them over. Sauté these for 3 to 4 minutes on each side, then pop them onto a holding dish. You might need to add a little more olive oil to the pan to fry the second batch.

When all the fritters are sautéed, pour your tomato sauce into the sauté pan and place over medium low heat. Twiddle with the flavor of the sauce if you want, more garlic, more basil whatever floats your boat. When the sauce is nice and warm slide the fritters back into the pan. Put a lid or cover on it, and cook VERY gently over very low heat for 20 minutes. Don't stir things around too much as the fritters will break up, just let them nestle in the sauce and heat through. Sprinkle the remaining Parmesan cheese over the top for the last two minutes of cooking then spoon onto warm plates and dive in.

Anna's Tomatoes
Makes 12

This recipe comes, word of mouth, from one of Felix's lovely little aunties……..

    2 cups fresh sourdough breadcrumbs
    6 large firm but ripe tomatoes
    1 cup finely grated Parmesan plus a little extra for topping
    1 large clove of garlic peeled and mashed
    1/2 cup fresh basil finely chopped
    Fresh black pepper

Pre-heat the oven to 375 degrees. Pop the breadcrumbs onto a baking sheet and toast for about 10 minutes. Stir them around once or twice so that they all brown evenly and don't turn your back on them or they will be charcoal. Leave the oven on.

Take your tomatoes and cut them in half horizontally. You can remove a little bit of the stem part it you like, but don't make too big a hole. With a spoon, scoop out the flesh of the tomato halves and deposit it into a bowl and set the shell of the tomato aside. To the flesh of the tomatoes add the toasted breadcrumbs, the cheese, the garlic and the basil and mix it around with your hands. It will be a lovely squishy mess. Season this with salt and pepper and then fill your tomato shells with it. Pop the filled shells onto a baking sheet and into the oven for about 25 to 30 minutes. After about 20 minutes, put the extra Parmesan on top and back into the oven to finish off. These are definitely best at room temperature.

Ratatouille

One big pot

This is great spooned over a thick chunk of oven baked halibut, or a grilled chicken breast. It's also great at room temperature with grilled bread (slathered with olive oil and garlic of course) and some good cheeses.

    4 tbsp olive oil
    1 sweet onion sliced
    2 cloves garlic peeled chopped and smashed
    1 red pepper seeded and cut into bite sized pieces
    1 green pepper seeded and cut into bite sized pieces
    4 stalks celery chopped
    2 zucchini cut in half lengthways and then sliced into ½ inch thick slices
    1 yellow squash cut in half lengthways and sliced into ½ inch thick slices
    1 small eggplant cut into 1" cubes
    1 36 oz can San Marzano Tomatoes chopped
    1/4 cup tomato puree
    1 tbsp dried oregano
    1 tsp dried parsley
    1 bay leaf
    1/2 cup capers drained
    1 cup black olives roughly chopped

Heat the olive oil in a large soup pot then sauté the onions, garlic, peppers, celery, zucchini, squash and eggplant for 4 to 5 minutes, stirring around frequently. Add the tomatoes and the tomato puree and also the dried herbs. Bring this up to almost a boil, then turn the heat down really low and simmer for 2 hours. Stir in the capers and olives about 10 minutes before it's done.

Scallions Leeks & Potatoes with Balsamic Vinaigrette

For 2 (as a side dish)

This was originally a recipe that used ramps, which are wild garlic greens, but my local grocery store has not heard of these, and there don't seem to be any growing wild in Bellevue, so I adapt.

> 6 small waxy potatoes (like Red Bliss, Fingerlings or Yukon Golds)
> 2 tbsp olive oil for frying
> 2 small leeks
> 4 scallions
> 1/4 cup water
> 1 tbsp balsamic vinegar
> 1 tsp lemon juice
> 1/4 cup olive oil

Cook the potatoes (whole) in boiling salted water until just tender when poked at with a knife. Drain and set aside to cool to room temperature. Trim tops and bottoms from leeks, remove tough outer leaves, slice them in half lengthways then wash them really well. Trim tops, bottoms and outer layer from the scallions but leave them whole. Heat the olive oil in a large sauté pan. Sauté the leeks and scallions for about 5-6 minutes, then add the water to the pan and continue to cook until they are soft and developing little brown spots. The water speeds up the cooking process considerably, and the leeks will be tough if they aren't fully cooked through. When the leeks and scallions are done to your liking, set them aside to cool.

I like to serve this on a large white, oval platter for some reason. Slice the cooled potatoes into 1/4" thick rounds and arrange in a thin layer all over the platter. Top with the sautéed leeks and scallions, scattered all around, and season with fresh black pepper. In a screw top jar, put the vinegar, lemon juice and olive oil and shake well to combine. Drizzle this over the platter of leeks and potatoes and serve at room temperature.

Eggplant Zucchini & Tomato Basil Gratin
For 4 (as a side dish or for 2 as a vegetarian main dish)

Like summer in a baking dish.

  1 large eggplant
  3 medium zucchini
  Olive oil for frying
  1 cup crushed tomatoes in puree
  1/2 cup Feta cheese crumbled (you could also use Parmesan, Mozzarella or Provolone)
  Fresh basil
  Black pepper
  Grated Parmesan for topping.

Wash and slice the eggplant into 1/4 inch rounds. Cut the ends off the zucchini, cut them in half lengthways and then slice into 1/4 inch thick slices lengthways. Heat a couple tablespoons of olive oil in a sauté pan over medium high heat. Fry the eggplant and zucchini in batches until they are just golden and soft, (add more oil to the pan as you need it), and set them aside on a plate to cool.

Heat the oven to 375 degrees. In a medium sized, oven proof baking dish put a layer of eggplant, then a layer of zucchini, then spread a couple spoons of the tomatoes over the top, sprinkle with a little cheese, tear a few leaves of basil over it, season with pepper, and then repeat the layers until all are used up. Cover with foil and bake for 1 hour. Uncover and sprinkle with Parmesan, then return to the oven for 5 minutes.

Braised Lettuce with Peas & Cream

For 2

Sounds a bit strange, tastes really great. I think it's a quirky little English dish, but I can't truly remember the origin of this one. It does sound like something English people would come up with though; especially in my part of England, where Devonshire cream is King........ and Queen as well. The true test of the deliciousness of this dish however, is that my Stepdad will eat it. He is not a vegetable lover, but the way he woofs this down, you'd think it was Haagen Daas.

2 heads of Romaine lettuce
2 tbsp butter
2 large shallots peeled and finely chopped
1 clove garlic peeled and mashed
1 tbsp dried marjoram
1 1/2 cups frozen peas
1/2 cup dry white wine
1/2 cup chicken stock
1/4 cup non fat sour cream
1/4 cup non fat half and half
Fresh cracked black pepper

Remove the outer leaves from the heads of lettuce until you are left with nice tight hearts. Heat the butter or margarine in a medium sauté pan. Add the shallots and garlic and sauté until just beginning to brown. Add the marjoram and the peas and stir about. Pour in the wine and stock, then stir in the creams. Bring this to a boil and place the whole hearts of lettuce into the pan. Turn the heat down to low and put a lid on the pan. Simmer for about 20 minutes, turning the heads of lettuce half way through. Keep an eye on the liquid level and add more wine, stock or water if it gets too thick. Be gentle with the lettuce you don't want it to fall apart. When the lettuce is all wilted and warmed through, transfer everything to a serving dish, grind some fresh pepper over it and off you go.

Roasted Cauliflower with Anchovy Breadcrumbs
For 4

Y̲ou just have to try this on people. There's no point in trying to explain anchovies and cauliflower. Don't tell 'em what you're serving, just spring it on them at the last minute.

1 cup breadcrumbs
1 whole head of cauliflower trimmed of green leaves.
4 tbsp olive oil
4 large anchovies finely chopped

Pre-heat the oven to 375 degrees. Line a baking sheet with non stick foil and spread the breadcrumbs over it in a thin layer. Toast for 10 minutes until golden brown and crisp. Not burnt, just crisp. You'll need to keep stirring them about to make sure they brown evenly. When golden, pour them into a bowl and let cool. Keep the foil on the baking sheet to roast the cauliflower on.

Set the cauliflower on its base and then cut it into 1" thick slices, going from top to bottom, with a serrated knife. Brush the slices all over with half of the olive oil and lay them on the baking sheet. Bake for 40 minutes until nice and soft and browned, turn the slices over half way through the cooking time. With your fingers, toss the finely chopped anchovies with the toasted breadcrumbs and the remainder of the olive oil. Sprinkle this over the top of the cauliflower slices and then bake for an additional 10 minutes.

Spinach Sage & White Bean Timbales

For 4

These really are easy to make, and timbales are something nobody ever does these days, so if you turn a few of these out, you will definitely get extra Brownie points. Maybe even your timbale badge.

    1 10 oz package chopped baby spinach thawed
    1 can white cannellini beans (do not drain)
    1 large clove garlic
    3 large fresh sage leaves finely chopped (or 1 tsp dried)
    1/2 cup finely grated Parmesan
    1/4 cup mascarpone cheese (cream cheese will work too)
    2 large eggs

Pre-heat the oven to 375 degrees. Squeeze all the water out of the spinach then combine all the ingredients in a food processor and blend for 1 minute. Scrape down the sides and blend again for 30 seconds.

Brush the insides of 4 ramekins with olive oil and then divide the bean mixture evenly between them. Set the ramekins in a deep baking dish and fill with hot water to come 2/3 of the way up their sides. Bake for 45 minutes or until a toothpick inserted in the middle of one comes out clean.

To serve, run a knife around the sides of the ramekins and invert them onto your plates.

Rosemary Garlic Potatoes
For 4

My stepmother makes the finest roast potatoes in the universe, and I cannot begin to claim such talent in the tuber department. She has freely shared her technique with me, but my attempts are never as perfectly golden crisp on the outside and succulent on the inside as hers. So I make this kind instead, and they are quite passable if hers are not on the menu.

16 baby red potatoes
1 good tsp crushed garlic
2 tbsp extra virgin olive oil
1 tbsp coarse ground Dijon mustard
1 large sprig of fresh rosemary
Fresh cracked black pepper

Wash and trim all the eyes and blemishes off the potatoes. Bring a small pot of salted water to a boil and pop in the tubers. Turn the heat down and gently boil them until just barely tender. About 10 – 15 minutes. Drain the potatoes and set aside to cool.

Line a baking sheet with non-stick foil. Take each potato and stick a small vegetable knife into it and twist gently to crack the potato open. This gives nice rough surfaces for the garlic and oil to stick to and get all golden brown in the oven.

Stir the garlic, the olive oil and mustard together and then toss the potatoes in it till they're all glossy. Tear off the whole leaves from the rosemary sprig and scatter over the top of the potatoes. Give them a generous grinding of pepper. You can hold them like this for several hours if you like, then they'll only take 10 to 15 minutes in a 400 degree oven to finish up. They should have nice crispy bits around the edges. I know, they're not like Sheila's....... but not bad.

Root Vegetable Gratin
For 4 - 6

This is a little different, sort of thinking outside the potato.

    1 large yam
    1 large rutabaga
    1 large parsnip
    3 large sprigs fresh thyme leaves removed
    Fresh cracked black pepper
    1 cup non fat chicken stock
    2 tsp butter
    1/2 cup non fat yogurt
    1/2 cup non fat sour cream
    1/2 cup finely grated Parmesan (or Swiss, or Cheddar or whatever you prefer)

Pre-heat the oven to 375 degrees. Peel and thinly slice the vegetables and put them into a 12" by 12" gratin dish in alternating layers. Sprinkle the thyme leaves over the top season with the black pepper and pour the chicken stock over. Dot the top with the butter and cover with non-stick foil. Pop into the oven for 30 to 40 minutes until veggies are cooked to the barely tender stage. Stir them about occasionally to make sure they all cook evenly. Don't be afraid of it, it doesn't all have to be in nice neat layers you know, no one's going to care....really!

When they are all pretty soft, pat them down into a nice even bed. Mix together the yogurt, sour cream and cheese, and pour over the gratin, smoosh around a bit, return the dish to the oven, uncovered, add another dusting of black pepper, then and bake until golden brown, about 20 minutes.

Eggplant Parmesan

For 2

Luscious, sweet eggplant, cheese, tomatoes basil.....what could possibly be better than this. Free, painless liposuction maybe?

>   2 medium eggplants
>   1/3 cup of olive oil
>   2 cups San Marzano tomato sauce with basil
>   1 ball fresh buffalo Mozzarella thinly sliced
>   1/2 cup grated Parmesan
>   Bunch of fresh basil
>   Fresh cracked black pepper

Pre-heat the oven to 375 degrees. Wash and slice your eggplant into 1/4 inch thick rounds. Line a couple of baking sheets with non-stick foil. Brush both sides of the eggplant rounds with the oil and put onto the baking sheets in a single layer. Pop into the oven for 10 - 12 minutes then flip them over and bake for 10 - 12 minutes more. When the eggplant rounds are all nice and soft and golden, remove them to a clean plate and let them cool a bit. If your eggplants are on the big side, you might need to use three baking sheets, or do it in batches.

Select a 12" square baking dish that you can take from oven to table and spread a thin layer of tomato sauce over the bottom. Now put in a single layer of the roasted eggplant slices and then spread a little more tomato sauce over the top. Next lay on a few pieces of the fresh mozzarella, then a sprinkle of Parmesan and two or three torn fresh basil leaves. Then repeat with another layer of eggplant etc. etc. Finish up with a cheese layer and cover with more non-stick foil. Pop into the 375 degree oven for about 35 minutes, then remove the foil cover and bake for 10 minutes more.

The Big 3 Holidays...
The Goose

You can drink eggnog till you're sick, and make the dog wear reindeer antlers, but as far as we English people are concerned, if December 25th doesn't involve a roast goose, it's not Christmas. There is no waffling on the subject, there is no wiggle room......it's practically the law, and being the law abiding English person that I am, I will go to great lengths to make sure there's a goose on my holiday table...... Some years, the lengths have been greater than others.

Thankfully, with a few mouse clicks and a sturdy credit card, fresh geese are easily come by these days, but it hasn't always been that way. Back in the dark ages, before Al Gore invented the internet, they used to be as hard to find as a suitable husband. You girls know how it goes, by the time you realize you want one, all the best ones are taken. Anyway, many years ago, as Christmas was approaching, I'd hunted down a fresh goose in our local liquor store. Well to be honest, it was the farmer who raised the goose who was in the liquor store, not the goose itself. He was browsing in the Wild Turkey section if I remember correctly, obviously a poultry man to the core. To cut a long story short, I paid the man his money, and he promised me a goose on Christmas Eve.

After dragging its feet a bit, Christmas Eve finally showed up, and I dispatched Felix, to pick up our goose. George (portly black Labrador) and I stayed behind to attend to some important Christmas Eve preparations. We'd managed to paint our toenails red, and one of us was modeling his reindeer antlers, when the crunch of gravel announced the return of the great white goose hunter. Excitedly, I flung open the door, and Felix staggered into the kitchen carrying The Goose.....complete with head, feet, feathers and everything. Even worse, the thing was still warm, having obviously waddled off this mortal coil just moments earlier. George, still wearing his antlers, was immediately seized by uncontrollable doggy lust. His eyes were telling him this was a dead goose, his nose was telling him this was a dead goose, and his deeply buried hunting genes were shrieking RETRIEVE, RETRIEVE. He doesn't know what retrieve means, but he did seem to know that dead geese are pretty important in the Labrador scheme of things.

While George was close to goose induced dementia, I was already there. I am an enthusiastic carnivore, but I live in complete denial when it comes to how my meat gets from farm to plate. Naked, headless poultry, under plastic wrap, I can deal with, but poultry that still has a face (and cute little webbed feet) is definitely a problem. It's the eyes you see. Anything that still has eyes cannot be Christmas dinner, and that's all there is to it.

"What shall I do with it" Felix whispered, as he stood on his tippy toes to keep the dangling neck from George the Reindog's retrieval efforts. "Just get it outside" I croaked, and he obediently wobbled off to the patio table. We stared miserably at the body for a minute, and then (with an indignant George in tow) headed for the kitchen, and the hot buttered rum. Well it was the shock you see, and anyway, I'm pretty sure it was noon somewhere.

Huddled in the kitchen, we sipped our rum, and studied the deceased through the frosty window. When the rum ran out, the body was still sprawled across the Lazy Susan, and appeared to have every intention of staying there. Then, just when things seemed at their darkest, I remembered my favorite quote from the great Bette Davis. **"There comes a time in every girl's life when the only thing that helps is a glass of Champagne."** Well this girl definitely needed help, so we opened a bottle of Veuve Cliquot to see if Bette was right.

Turns out Ms. Davis was spot on, because gradually, things did begin to look a little brighter......then a lot brighter, and eventually......hysterically funny. Buoyed by the bubbly, and ready to pluck, we headed outside.

Slowly, at first, then faster, the feathers started to fly. George had come completely unglued by this time; chasing tumbling feathers, and muttering excitedly under his doggy breath. **" See, this isn't so bad; we should do this every year."** Felix remarked as he leaned in to grip another handful of feathers.......The goose chose that moment to honk.....loudly......twice. George went barking into orbit, and I shot backwards and landed on my rear. Felix just stood there, feathers drifting around him, staring in mute horror at the half naked goose. After a full minute of round-eyed disbelief, common sense prevailed. Our plucking efforts had forced air over the goose's still intact vocal cords, producing a posthumous honk. Weak with relief that we were not going to do jail time for goose cruelty, we finished the Champagne (and the plucking), and waited for George to re-enter the atmosphere.

He did splash down eventually, but was pretty much a space cadet for the rest of the day. Like all good Christmas stories, this one has a happy ending; the goose was delicious, and the space cadet scored the parson's nose.

Very Juicy Thanksgiving Pear Brined Turkey
For 4 (with lots of good leftovers)

Time for big family dinners, and big family fights. You know what I mean….. "If Uncle Roger mentions the hamster incident one more time, I'm going to take a baseball bat to his Cadillac." That sort of thing.

If you think about it, it's a really good job that turkey puts people to sleep, because I'm sure it has prevented some bloody family massacres and vandalized Cadillacs over the years. It's pretty hard to swing a Louisville Slugger with any momentum when all you really want to do is nap. Mmmmmmm…..tranquilizer with gravy.

For Brine and Turkey
4 quarts pear juice divided (1 quart, 1/2 cup and remainder)
1 cup sea salt
6 large bay leaves
1 tbsp black peppercorns
1 tbsp allspice berries
4 quarts water
1 large cooler (about 20 quarts) or a large pot which will hold the turkey, totally submerged in liquid)
1 14 lb turkey (fresh or defrosted)
2 tbsp butter, melted

For Sage Gravy
6 cups cold water
8 fresh sage leaves
1/2 large onion chopped
1 stalk celery chopped
1 large carrot chopped
Turkey giblets (not the liver)
1/2 cup pear juice (saved from the above 4 qts)
1 tsp cornstarch

For Sausage Sage and Onion Stuffing
3 mild Italian sausages
4 cups coarse bread torn into small pieces
1 medium onion peeled and finely chopped
1 large pear peeled cored and chopped
3 tbsp dried sage crumbled
1 cup milk
Fresh cracked black pepper

In a small pot, simmer the 1 quart of the pear juice with the salt, bay leaves and peppercorns for about 5 minutes, then take off the heat and cool completely.

Into the large (very clean) cooler pour the remaining pear juice (except for the 1/2 cup) the 4 quarts of water and the now completely cooled salt/juice mix. Get your turkey out of his bag and remove the giblets and any excess fat you see hanging around. Keep the giblets for gravy. Wash him in cold water, inside and out and dunk him into the cooler full of pear brine. I put mine outside as it's cold at Thanksgiving here, and he's in a cooler with a lid, but you can put him in the fridge in a big pot if you want. In the morning, nice and early, get him out of the brine and pat him dry. Then leave him on a plate in the fridge, uncovered, until you're ready to roast.

In a small saucepan combine all the above gravy ingredients, cover, bring to a boil, then simmer very gently for two hours. Drain the liquid into a small saucepan and discard the giblets and veggies, or in my case, let Felix eat them. Take the last half cup of pear juice and stir in the cornstarch. Add this to the turkey giblet stock and bring to a boil. Turn the heat down and simmer until the gravy is reduced and thickened to your liking. Then turn off the heat. You can re-warm the gravy while the turkey is resting and being carved by the man of the house.

Cook the sausages however you like; microwave, sauté, bake, doesn't matter, then cool and cut them into small chunks. Put the cooled sausages, bread, onion, pear and sage into a large mixing bowl and mix with your hands. Pour in the milk and mix again until all the mixture is wet.

Pre-heat the oven to 350 degrees. Stuff the turkey loosely with the stuffing and tie his legs together. Put him on a rack in a roasting dish and pop into the oven for an hour. After an hour, put foil over the really brown bits and baste the rest with the melted butter. Keep checking on him and basting with the butter. After 2 hours, put foil over the whole bird and roast for about 1 more hour. Thermometer in inner thigh should read 175 degrees. When you have achieved this number, get him out of the oven and put a tent of foil over and let him rest 30 minutes before carving.

Christmas Goose

For 4 (with a few leftovers…..geese are a bit skinnier than turkeys)

Christmas morning in Britaly: Kick off is about 10:30 a.m. with piping hot Italian sausages nestled in warm, crispy bread rolls, and a nice bottle of Veuve Cliquot. Then there is present opening by the fire. This is followed by the inevitable fashion show.......despite the fact that nothing looks good with pajamas or bunny slippers. Then, when we have completely pillaged the tree and the living room is a sea of knotted ribbon and shredded Christmas wrap....... we cook The Goose!

1 fresh goose 10 to 12 lbs (naked)
4 tbsp olive oil
2 chopped carrots
1 large chopped onion
2 sticks chopped celery
4 cups chicken stock
2 cups dry white wine
Small bunch Italian (flat leaf) parsley
6 whole cloves
2 bay leaves
1 bunch fresh thyme
1/2 cup of brandy
1/3 cup plus 2 tbsp red currant jelly

Pull off any extra bits of fat you find hanging around the goose and discard. (Would that this was possible with saddle bags and tummies.) Cut off the first two bony joints of the wings. Wash him all over, pat dry with paper towels and then tie his legs together with butcher's string. Prick the skin all over with a sharp knife, or a skewer, and set him aside for a minute.

Add the olive oil to the largest French oven, very deep roasting pan, or stock pot that you have. (It has to be large enough to completely contain the goose.) Heat the oil over moderately high heat, and then add the carrots, onions, celery and the giblets from the goose if you have them. (Hold the liver for the dog.) Sauté until the vegetables are brown, then add the stock, wine, bay leaves and other herbs. Now put your goose into this stock and add water until the bird is submerged. Cover the pot or whatever you're using, and keeping it at a very gentle simmer, cook for 1 1/2 hours. Then turn the goose to make sure all portions are cooked under the poaching liquid equally, and let it simmer for another 1 1/2 hours. Let it cool slightly and then fish him out of the poaching liquid. (**Don't throw poaching liquid out.**) You can stuff goose with your choice of stuffing at this point if you so desire. I usually use the sage and onion one from the previous recipe, but I omit the sausage as goose is richer than turkey and I like to keep the stuffing lighter.

Heat the oven to 425 degrees. Put goose, breast side up, on a rack, in a roasting pan. Mix the 2 tbsp red currant jelly with 1 tbsp hot water and brush all over the goose. Then roast him for about 30 to 40 minutes in the hot oven. You can baste him again with more currant jelly glaze after 20 minutes or so. While the goose is roasting, strain the poaching liquid and then put 4 cups of it back into the French oven or soup pot, if you are watching your weight, put the poaching liquid in a fat separator and use only the stock. Now add the brandy and the 1/3 cup of redcurrant jelly to the four cups of poaching liquid, and then simmer the liquid until it is reduced by half. (You can thicken with a little cornstarch if you prefer a thicker gravy.) Season to taste, with salt and pepper, and keep warm until you carve the goose.

When the goose has roasted for 30 or 40 minutes, and is browned to your liking remove from the oven and put a tent of aluminum foil over him, and leave him to sit for at least 15 minutes before you carve. Remember to serve the gravy on the side.

I like to serve roast goose with traditional English accompaniments, like the above-mentioned pear, sage and onion stuffing, roasted onions and potatoes and Brussels sprouts with crispy bacon and cream. That's definitely a Merry Christmas.

New Year's Roast Beast

For 4 (very hungry people and maybe a sandwich or two)

I sent Felix to buy the prime rib roast one year, and he came back with a 10 ribber........for the two of us. In case you have never seen a 10 rib roast, just imagine half a cow without the legs. It was so impressive, we took photographs of it being magnificent on the kitchen table, and proudly put them in our photo album for the year.......right after the Christmas morning pictures of me wearing the Barcelino silk suit with the bunny slippers.

Sadly though, we knew that even Felix couldn't eat that much beef, and we reluctantly cut it in two and consigned one piece to the freezer. The other half went on to be a fabulous piece of roast beast though.......and a quarter of a cow turned out to be quite enough for 2 people.

> 1/4 cup of garlic paste from a jar
> 2 tbsp olive oil
> 1 tbsp herbs de Provence
> Fresh black pepper
> Sea salt
> 1 bone in rib roast trimmed of excess fat (5 or 6 bones should do it)
> 1 cup dry red wine
> 1/2 cup low sodium beef stock

Put the garlic paste into a small bowl and add the olive oil and herbs de Provence. Stir together until you have a nice soft paste then season with pepper and salt.

Take the oven up to 450 degrees. Put the rib roast into a roasting dish, concave, rib side down. Slather the garlic herb mix over the top and season the roast with some more salt and pepper. Pour the red wine and beef stock into the roasting pan (not right over the meat or you'll wash all the garlic off) and pop into the oven for 20 minutes. Turn the heat down to 350 degrees and roast until the center of the roast is 140 degrees (for a rare roast). Let sit at least 5 minutes before carving.

Serve with lots of hot horseradish for garnish and the juices from the pan.

Strawberries & Other Sweeties...

I will never be able to look at a strawberry and not fondly remember George the Wonderdog daintily picking his own.....

The Bark Brothers

For the first time in our lives, Felix and I are alone, and we have white carpet. Yeeee haaaaa! No kids, no dogs, no cats, no chickens, no horses. Well, technically I suppose, we do still have the dogs......they're in cute little urns in Felix's office, being used as bookends........and very good bookends they are too.

They were both amazing boys, and I feel very privileged to have been owned by them for more than 13 wonderful years. George was a black Labrador, Vince was a Doberman. Both were blithering idiots, comedians, escape artists, pigs, trouble, expensive, irreplaceable, love machines. They also thought they were great guard dogs. It didn't really matter that they were complete charlatans and could no more harm a fly than go without dinner, but boy could they bark the bark.

Back in the days of the aforementioned menagerie, Felix and I lived on 10 completely fenced acres and the Bark Brothers diligently patrolled it all: horse pastures, chicken coop, barns, vegetable gardens and flower beds, nothing was left unattended for long. One thing was certain, no one was going to make off with a zucchini or a zinnia on their watch. George was CEO (Chief Escape Officer) and perfectly capable of picking his own strawberries, Vince was Vice President of Mischief and incapable of everything except slobber production and shedding. They were inseparable.........but it hadn't always been that way...George's nose was so far out of joint the day we brought puppy Vince home, he would have nothing to do with any of us. There he sat, stiff with indignation on the far side of the lawn, back towards us, spare tires rolling gently down over his doggy knees. Every time we tried to bring the puppy to meet him, he would sigh, heave himself up and plod off to the other side of the lawn, disgusted at this revolting turn of events. By dint of sheer enthusiasm and being too dim to know he wasn't welcome, Vince finally wore him down and by the end of the week George had assumed the role of mother hen and mentor. **"This is how you eat a corndog stick boy......or, nope you can't chase that particular cat, it's one of ours"**.........that sort of thing.

Felix and I never told anyone that the boys were buffoons, and we tried desperately to perpetuate the myth that they were in fact bonafide guard dogs and not to be trifled with. It made us feel safer, living way out there in the boonies and all that. The myth was frequently shattered however, like the day I was out on the front lawn explaining to the heating oil delivery man (on the other side of the fence) that although they were hurtling up and down the fence line, salivating like wild hyenas and kicking up the most ungodly din, the dogs would in fact not hurt him…… as long as I was in attendance. Still looking rather dubious about his safety, oil man climbed gingerly over the fence with his hose, while I held the barkers at bay. Delivery completed, he hastened back to the dogless side of the fence, and I released the slavering beasts to resume their nonsense. At that very moment……. with the dogs at the peak of their performance, the meter reader man arrived, got out of his van, swung open the gate and came into the yard. I saw the oil delivery man's eyes widen as he watched the boys hurtle across the lawn in full cry, slobber flying. Surely the man would be torn to shreds, never to read another meter again………. **"George….. Vince, you old devils, how's it going?"** the meter reader said as he handed out puppy cookies, scratched ears and accepted multiple doggy kisses. The oil man promised me he wouldn't tell anyone.

George may have been the brains of the outfit, but Vince, when fully grown, was definitely the muscle. He looked cold, hard and menacing, and when full grown, he weighed more than me, no mean feat I can tell you. The fact that he was afraid of our cats, would sit on your lap if you were stupid enough to let him, and slept with a teddy bear, was not immediately apparent to those not in the know.

One summer we had two Mexican gentlemen come to do some irrigation repair in the vegetable garden. The Bark Brothers were on patrol elsewhere on the grounds, and for a while, they were blissfully unaware that there were intruders on their property. I was standing chatting to the workmen, and explaining what needed to be done, when I glanced across the horse pasture, and saw that Vince had spotted us. He froze, with one front paw lifted……. stared…….looked back at George for permission to launch….. and then hurled himself across the field like a werewolf on speed. I seem to remember that everything went into slow motion at that point. One of the men turned to see what I was looking at and beheld the awful vision of Vince racing toward him at full throttle. I'd never seen a grown man throw himself over a six foot chain link fence before, in fact I wouldn't have thought it was possible if I hadn't seen two of them do it with my own eyes. They were, of course, in no danger of being attacked, although given Vince's lack of braking ability, they might have been taken out like bowling pins and given a nasty licking.

Of all their antics though, their ritual response to the daily drive by of the red pick up truck was probably the funniest. Why the red pick up?.... you might inquire. Well, this was because Spot, the neighbor dog, rode in the back of said red pick-up. The truck would always come from the bottom of the road, roar past our little farm and disappear up the hill. The boys waited anxiously for this magic moment every day. One of them would spot the red truck turning the corner, and would sound the alarm. Vince would then commence doing laps up and down the fence line at 90 miles an hour, barking his fool head off. George would join in at about 30 miles an hour, a more dignified speed for a dog in his position, but giving equal effort in the barking department. Given the different speeds of the players, some collisions were inevitable, but Vince was fairly adept at hurdling George if their paths crossed, and IF he happened to be looking where he was galloping at the time. If not, George would bite the dust. At each end of the fence line was a completely destroyed patch of lawn where they made their tumble turns amid flying grass and gravel from the driveway. All this time of course, Spot would be hanging over the side of the truck, ears and tongue flying, barking back at them like a dog possessed. It was obviously their idea of sheer heaven, as they nearly expired from joy every time it happened.

As the years went by and George got a little slower, he'd let Vince do the laps solo, while he handled the back up barking. Vince liked it because he could crank it up to 100 miles an hour without George in the way………and it still seemed to work for Spot too.

172

Not a day goes by that I don't still miss the idiots terribly ………but they'd be hell on this white carpet.

Balsamic Macerated Strawberries with Mascarpone Ice Cream
For 4

As perfect a combination as dramatic eyes and nude lips.

> 1 pint strawberries
> 3 tbsp balsamic vinegar
> 3 tbsp superfine sugar
> Mascarpone ice cream (if you can find it, if not, vanilla or dulce de leche are good)
> 2 amaretti cookies

Wash and hull the strawberries then slice them however you like. Combine the vinegar and sugar and when well mixed and the sugar is dissolved, pour over the strawberries. Toss them around well, cover and leave to macerate in the fridge for about 2 hours.

Serve in nice big martini glasses. Divide the ice cream between the glasses, then top with the berries and accumulated juices. Crumble the amaretti cookies and sprinkle over the tops.

Gooseberry Fool

For 4

Any foolish kind of fruit you have on hand will do really; pears, peaches, plums etc.

    2 cups canned gooseberries in light syrup
    1/2 split vanilla bean
    1 tsp fresh lemon zest
    3/4 cup heavy cream
    1 tbsp confectioner's sugar
    Dark chocolate curls for garnish

Drain the gooseberries and reserve the syrup. Put syrup into a small saucepan and add the vanilla bean and lemon zest. Bring to a boil and reduce until you have 1/4 cup, then take off heat and cool to room temp. Put gooseberries into a blender and puree until smooth.

In a separate bowl, beat the cream until it just holds soft peaks, then add the sugar and 3 tbsp of the gooseberry syrup and beat again until just combined.

Take four wineglasses and divide half of the gooseberry puree between them, top each with a layer of the whipped cream (use half). Divide the rest of the gooseberry puree over the top of this and finish them with the rest of the cream. Drizzle the last tablespoon of the gooseberry syrup over the top and refrigerate for at least 1 hour before serving. Garnish with the chocolate curls unless you have already eaten them while waiting for the fools to cool.

Individual Lemon Soufflés
For 6

Soufflés are actually easier than you think, especially little ones. The big ones can be mean and subversive I will admit.

    Butter and superfine sugar to prepare ramekins
    3/4 cup non fat milk + 1 tbsp
    3/4 cup superfine sugar
    3 1/2 tbsp cornstarch
    3 large egg yolks
    2 tbsp fresh lemon juice
    2 tbsp lemon curd
    1 tbsp grated lemon zest
    5 large egg whites
    Flaked almonds for garnish

Pre-heat oven to 400 degrees. Take six ramekins and rub their insides with some of the butter and then coat the inside with a little of the sugar. Put the milk into a saucepan over medium heat and bring to a simmer. In a medium bowl whisk together 1/4 cup of the sugar, the cornstarch and the egg yolks until well blended. When the milk is just hot gradually whisk it into the egg yolk mix in the bowl. Return the whole lot to the saucepan and bring back to a simmer, keep whisking all the time. This is custard we're making people. When it comes to a simmer, remove from the heat and whisk in the lemon juice, curd and the zest. Set this aside in the saucepan and allow to cool. Keep stirring it about now and then so it doesn't form too much of a skin.

When the custard mixture is cool, beat the egg whites in a bowl until they form soft peaks, then add the remaining half cup of sugar and beat some more until they are stiff, but don't go over the line and make them dry. Fold the whites very carefully into the lemon/egg custard then spoon into the prepared ramekins. Scatter a few flaked almonds over the top of each soufflé and then bake until just lightly browned on top for about 18 - 20 minutes. Now rush them smartly to the table and serve….before they prove me wrong and collapse on you.

Baked Stuffed Peaches
For 4

Harder to resist than the Nordstrom half yearly sale…..and a lot cheaper.

    1 cup of walnuts
    5 tablespoons of brown sugar
    2 large egg yolks
    1 tsp vanilla essence
    4 firm peaches
    1/3 cup seedless blackberry jam

Pre-heat the oven to 400 degrees. Grind the walnuts until very fine, in a food processor. Add 4 tablespoons of the sugar, the egg yolks and vanilla and pulse until combined. Halve and pit the peaches and place them cut side up on a baking sheet. Fill the peach halves with the walnut mixture, mounding it up a bit. Sprinkle with the remaining sugar and bake in the oven until golden brown. This should take about 12 to 15 minutes.

While peaches are baking put the blackberry jam in a small saucepan and warm gently until it gets all runny. Serve with really good vanilla ice cream and the warmed jam drizzled over the tops.

Frangipane Pear & Hazelnut Tart
One 14" Tart

Okay, this one probably breaks the KISS rule, but I saw a picture of a tart like this in a magazine many years ago and was totally smitten by its beauty. I couldn't help myself so I tweaked several different recipes over the years and came up with this version which looks absolutely fabulous, and doesn't take too much effort. I'm sorry, but every recovering Domestic Goddess has a relapse now and again. If you decide to try it, trust me, its beauty is droolworthy and it will do wonders for your culinary reputation.

For the Pastry
2 cups flour
1/2 cup superfine sugar
1 1/2 cups butter (very very cold)
2 egg yolks
1 tsp lemon juice
1 tbsp iced water

For the Frangipane
1 cup hazelnuts
1/2 cup sugar
1/4 cup flour
3/4 stick of butter
2 large eggs
1 tsp vanilla extract

And Also
1/4 cup quince preserves (use apricot or pear preserves/jam if you can't find quince)
3 firm but ripe pears

Combine the flour and sugar in a large mixing bowl and then cut the butter into the mixture with a sharp knife. Rub the butter into the flour with your fingers or a pastry mixer, whatever you like, even a food processor will do the job. Add the egg yolks, lemon juice and water and very gently stir this around with a metal spoon or fork. Now knead the mixture together with your fingers into a dough ball, do this very very gently and do not whatever you do maul it or overwork it in any way. Flatten the ball into a disk, wrap it in cling wrap and allow to rest in the fridge for at least an hour. (You can cheat and buy pastry if you like, but it has to be a sweet pastry for this to taste right.)

Pre-heat the oven to 375 degrees. After the dough has rested, remove from fridge and roll out to a large circle about 15" in diameter. Drape this over a shallow, 14" fluted tart pan, with a removable bottom and press gently to fit the pan. Trim the excess pastry by rolling a rolling pin over the top of the tart pan. Prick the bottom of the pie crust with a fork and then chill for 20 minutes in the fridge. Line the pie crust with grease proof paper and weight down with dried peas/beans or pie weights. Bake for about

20 minutes until the edges are just golden, then remove the weights and paper and bake for 10 minutes more. Remove from the oven and cool.

Toast the hazelnuts on a baking sheet for about 10 to 12 minutes or until just starting to brown. Shake them about a bit now to brown them evenly. You'll smell them all lovely and toasty when they're done. Cool the hazelnuts a bit and then roll them in a clean towel to remove the skins as much as possible. Put the toasted, skinned nuts into a food processor with 1/4 cup of the sugar and pulse until they are finely ground, then add the flour and pulse again to mix.

In a mixing bowl beat together the butter and the remaining 1/4 cup of sugar. Add the eggs one at a time and beat in well, add the vanilla extract and then stir in the nut/flour mixture gently until just combined. This is the frangipane bit.

Reduce the oven heat to 350 degrees. Spread the frangipane paste evenly into the tart shell. Put the quince preserves into a small saucepan and place over gentle heat so that it just melts a little and gets a bit thinner. Cut the pears in half lengthways, then in quarters. Peel and core the quarters and then slice them lengthways into 1/4 inch thick slices. Arrange the slices, slightly overlapping, in a circular pattern, all facing one way, starting from the outside and working towards the middle. You will end up with a nice rosette. Pop into the oven for about 35 minutes, the pears will brown lightly and the frangipane paste will puff up around them. Remove from the oven and brush the slightly melted quince preserves over the top of the pear slices, avoiding the frangipane paste. This will make it look all lovely and shiny........ fresh from a Parisian deli.

White Chocolate Mousse with Blackberries

For 4

I don't care if it's not really chocolate, I adore the white stuff, and can eat my body weight in it if left unsupervised.

    1 cup frozen blackberries plus 4 extra for garnish
    1/4 cup sugar
    9 ozs excellent quality white chocolate
    2 tbsp water
    1 3/4 cups chilled heavy cream
    1 tsp vanilla

Combine the blackberries and sugar in a saucepan and gradually bring to a simmer. Keep it simmering, stirring frequently, until you have a nice sauce. Puree the sauce in a food processor and then and strain into a bowl to remove the seeds. Cover and refrigerate.

Combine the white chocolate and the water in the top of a double boiler or a bowl set over a saucepan of gently boiling water. Stir this around until the chocolate is all melted, then remove from heat and let it rest for 10 minutes.

Put the 1/4 cup of cream and vanilla into a large bowl and then stir in the melted chocolate. Beat the rest of the whipping cream in a separate bowl until it forms stiff peaks, then gently fold the cream into the chocolate mixture. Spoon the mixture into martini glasses, cover with cling wrap and allow then to set up in the fridge for at least 2 hours. When ready to serve drizzle some blackberry sauce over the top and garnish with a whole blackberry and a small, clean blackberry leaf.

Rhubarb Crème Brulee
For 6

A terribly unappreciated fruit I feel, and an unexpected addition to the usual burnt cream. These need to chill out in the fridge for at least 4 hours so give yourself plenty of time.

For the Custard
5 large egg yolks
1/3 cup sugar
Pinch of salt
2 cups heavy cream
1 tsp vanilla

Also
1 cup canned rhubarb, drained and finely chopped

For the Sugar Topping
1/2 cup brown sugar
1/4 granulated sugar
(You can use regular old brown sugar if you don't have time to fiddle around with this)

Pre-heat the oven to 325 degrees. Whisk the egg yolks, the 1/3 cup of sugar and the pinch of salt until well combined. Put the cream into a medium saucepan and add the vanilla essence to it. Heat the cream but do not boil it. When hot, add slowly to the egg yolks, whisking all the time. Divide the rhubarb between 6 half cup, ovenproof ramekins, then top with the custard. Put the ramekins into a deep roasting pan and fill with water until the water level comes at least half way up the ramekins. Pop into the oven and bake until just set. This will take 35 to 40 minutes. Take the custards out of the oven, out of the water bath, and cool them on a rack. When the custards are cool, chill them in the fridge, uncovered, for at least four hours.

Turn the oven off, spread the brown sugar and the granulated sugar on a parchment lined baking sheet and pop into the oven to dry for about an hour. Then cool and whiz in a food processor until very fine.

When ready to serve, sprinkle the sugar over the tops of the custards and pop under a hot broiler until the sugar is caramelized, about 2 to 3 minutes, or you can use a fancy blow torch if you have one. Watch it like a hawk and turn if necessary to brown evenly. Serve immediately.

Lemon Poppy Seed Biscotti
Makes about 20

Addictive and dunkable. Not the toothbreakers sold at Costco. As the wife of a proud Italian, I quickly learned to make good biscotti, as grotty biscotti are grounds for divorce. You can substitute all kinds of things for the lemon and poppy seeds, for example, toasted almonds, dried cranberries, macadamia nuts and white chocolate chunks to name but a few.

2 cups flour
1 1/2 tsp baking powder
1/4 tsp salt
1/2 cup unsalted butter softened
1/4 cup sugar
2 eggs lightly beaten
1 tsp vanilla extract
Zest of 1 lemon finely grated
2 tbsp poppy seeds

Sift together flour, baking powder and salt in a small bowl. Cream butter and sugar in another large bowl until light and fluffy, then beat in eggs and vanilla. Add the lemon zest and poppy seeds then gradually add the flour mixture and combine, the dough will be very stiff, even to the point where you need to use your hands.

Transfer dough to a lightly floured surface and shape into a long flattened roll about 5" x 14" x 1". Line a baking sheet with non stick foil and transfer the flattened roll to baking sheet. Bake in the middle of a 350 degree oven until just golden brown, about 25 minutes. Remove from oven and set aside until cool enough to handle, about 15 mins. Using a serrated knife, cut the roll into 1/2" thick slices. Place slices cut side down on baking sheet and pop back into the oven for 5 minutes, then turn them over and bake for 5 minutes more. Do not overbake. Biscotti will feel a bit soft when you pull them out, but will become crisper and harder as they cool. Allow to cool completely on a wire rack. They will keep for up to 4 weeks in an airtight container, but not in my house.

After Eight Brownies
Makes 16

This is a construction idea I borrowed from Maida Heatter, the "Queen of Baking". Who else would have thought of mint chocs in the middle of brownies. She likes those Peppermint Patties, but I prefer After Eight Mints, which are, I think, more elegant.

No point making a smaller batch because these are just about as irresistible as Johnny Depp. If you're in a hurry, like for example when you hear "Mum, I need something for our bake sale at school tomorrow" and it's 10'o'clock on a Monday night, use a good brownie mix, and you're golden. I keep telling you, it's your kitchen, and they won't care anyway, they're kids.

> 1 cup walnuts
> 7 oz of the best bittersweet dark chocolate you can find (Vahlrona or Lindt are good)
> 1/4 cup Nutella (chocolate hazelnut spread)
> 1 stick of unsalted butter
> 1/2 cup all purpose flour
> 1/4 tsp salt
> 1/2 tsp baking powder
> 1/2 cup sugar
> 2 large eggs
> 1 box After Eight Mints (Any thin mint chocolates will do if you can't find these)

Pre-heat the oven to 350 degrees. Butter and flour a 9" square baking pan. Lightly toast the walnuts in the oven for about 10 minutes then cool and chop them.

Chop the chocolate into small pieces and place in a double boiler, or a bowl set over a saucepan of gently simmering water, along with the Nutella and butter. While the chocolate mixture melts, sift together the flour, salt and baking powder. Whisk the sugar into the melted chocolate and then add the eggs. Whisk this over the simmering water until it looks glossy. Take off the heat and stir in the flour mixture and the chopped walnuts only mixing until just combined.

Pour 1/2 of the batter into the baking pan and then unwrap your After Eight Mints and place them in a layer over the top of the batter. Pour the other 1/2 of the batter over the top and pop into the oven for 35 to 40 minutes or until a toothpick inserted comes out clean.

Sour Cream Pumpkin Cheesecake
One 9" Pie

I cannot stay out of this pie any more than I can stay out of the Nordstrom shoe department. As if caught in a Star Trek tractor beam, I am helpless to resist either one.

For Crust
2 cups digestive biscuit crumbs or (graham cracker)
1/3 cup melted butter

For Filling
2 8 oz packages of non fat cream cheese (room temp)
1 8 oz pot of Mascarpone cheese (room temp)
1 15 oz can solid pack pumpkin
1 cup of eggbeaters, or 4 large eggs beaten
1 cup sugar
1 tsp cinnamon
1 tsp nutmeg
1 tsp mace

For Toppings
16 oz pot of non fat sour cream
1 tbsp sugar
1 tsp vanilla essence

For Garnish
1 cup heavy whipping cream
1 tsp sugar
Dark chocolate shavings or curls

Pre-heat the oven to 350 degrees. Put biscuit crumbs in a small bowl and add the melted butter. Stir well then press onto the bottom of a 9" springform pan, bring the crumbs about an inch up the sides as well.

In a large mixing bowl put the cream cheese, Mascarpone and pumpkin and then using an electric mixer or a lot of elbow grease, beat until fluffy. Add the eggs gradually beating until just combined then add sugar and spices and beat again until just combined. Pour into the prepared crust and bake in the center of the oven for 1 hour and 45 minutes. Keep an eye on the thing, because ovens tend to vary. You can gently shake the pan now and again to see how set the "cake" is. It will not be completely set when you take it out of the oven, but it will continue to set up as it cools.

Bring pan out of oven and set on a rack. Don't turn the oven off. In a bowl mix the sour cream, sugar and vanilla. Smooth the sour cream mixture evenly over the top of the "cake" and bake for 10 minutes more. Take cake out of oven again and set on a rack to cool completely. Chill in the refrigerator overnight.

Just before you're ready to serve, whip the heavy cream with the sugar until it holds stiff peaks. Then spoon, or pipe, dollops around the edge of the cheesecake. Garnish with grated chocolate curls.

Figgy (Christmas) Pudding
For 6 (generously)

Pyromania on a plate. Needs a 5 cup pudding bowl that you can fit into a large pot of water to steam the pudding. You can make 2 smaller puds if you so choose.

    1 cup dried figs
    1/2 cup water
    1/4 cup Brandy
    1/2 cup dried apricots
    1 stick unsalted butter
    1 cup dark brown sugar
    2 large eggs
    1/2 tsp vanilla extract
    3/4 cup raisins
    3/4 cup sultanas (golden raisins)
    1 1/2 cups flour
    1 1/2 tsp baking powder (buy a new pot, don't use the 5 year old stuff at the back of your cupboard)
    Pinch of salt
    1 cup milk
    2 tbsp sugar free apricot jam
    1/4 cup Brandy
    Holly sprig
    Matches
    Heavy whipping cream for drizzling

Put 2/3 of the figs in a saucepan and add the water and the Brandy, bring to a boil then simmer for about 15 minutes. Puree the result in a food processor and set aside.

Put the remaining figs and apricots in a small bowl and cover with boiling water. Soak the fruit like this until plump (20 minutes) and then drain and set aside.

Coat the inside of a 5 cup pudding bowl with butter and cut a circle of parchment paper to fit over the top. It should be several inches bigger than the circumference of the bowl, so it will drape down over the sides.

In a large bowl, beat the butter and sugar until well creamed together. Add the eggs one at a time and beat in. Add the vanilla and the fig puree and beat in. Fold in the raisins and sultanas. Sift together the flour and baking powder and add the pinch of salt. Add half of the flour mixture to the fruit mixture and stir in, then add half of the milk and stir in. Add the last of the flour mix and stir in and then add the rest of the milk and stir in.

Spoon the apricot jam into the bottom of the pudding bowl. Arrange the soaked fruit on the bottom and a little ways up the sides of the bowl, then pour in the pudding batter. Cover the top with the parchment and secure with a hefty rubber band or string. Cover this with aluminum foil and another rubber band or more string.

Get your large pot and pop the pud in. If you have a rack or trivet to set the bowl on it will make less noise as it steams and will not make a mark on the bottom of your pot. I am not that organized and just stick it straight in the pot. Trivet or not, fill the pot with boiling water until it comes no more than 2/3 of the way up the sides of the pudding bowl. Put a lid on the pot, but leave it slightly ajar so steam can escape, and simmer this gently for about 2 hours. If an inserted toothpick comes out clean, with no raw pudding hanging on it, you can be sure the pud is done.

I always make the pud ahead of time, then just refrigerate it. Once Christmas dinner is over, I just re-steam it for 30 minutes before serving. This way you don't have a burner tied up for 2 hours while you're trying to cook the Turkey.

To serve the pudding after it is re-steamed, uncover it and turn it out onto a serving plate, pop a holly sprig on top, then pour the last 1/4 cup of Brandy over the top. Now turn all the lights out and carefully set light to the brandy. Just wave a match in the general direction and it will catch just fine. Carry pudding proudly to the table, taking care not to trip over dog, drop pudding and set light to Aunt Harriet. Blow out the flames, turn up the lights and serve big wedges drizzled with heavy cream.

P.S. Don't eat the holly.

Croquembouche
Enough to get at least 8 – 10 people sticky

Spectacular for a New Years Eve feast, and very fun to demolish. Again, this is just assembly really. To make profiteroles oneself would absolutely violate the KISS rule.

> 1 tub cream filled profiteroles (Costco has them……sorry about the biscotti remark)
> 2 cups sugar
> 1/2 cup water
> 1 10" cake board

Stir the sugar and water together in a heavy bottomed saucepan then bring to a boil. Once at a boil, stop stirring and switch to just swirling. Cook the syrup over moderate heat until it begins to turn a caramel color. Keep swirling and take it off the heat. It will continue to color and thicken. When it is like corn syrup, return it to the burner, but over very very low heat, do not let it simmer.

Seize your cakeboard and get ready to assemble. This is going to be a cone of cream puffs. Dip the bottom of each puff in the caramel (which should still be not simmering on the very low burner) and then "glue" to the edge of the board in a ring. Keep dipping the puffs' bottoms in the caramel and form a second, slightly smaller ring on top of the first. Let this dry a bit and then repeat with ever smaller rings until you can top the thing with just one puff. Do let the rings set up a bit before you start on the next one. When you have your cone, remove the caramel from the heat entirely and allow to cool until it is like molasses. Now comes the good bit. Dip the tip of a small spoon in the caramel and drizzle all over the croquembouche. Keep drizzling until you have a gauzy caramel shell over the whole thing.

This should be served as soon as possible, but it will hold for a couple of hours if necessary. To serve, use the back of a spoon to shatter the caramel cage and dismantle one puff at a time.

Snapshots from Britaly...

It does rain in Britaly sometimes... But we don't care

Home of the Stilton Bake

from this...

...to this! Look mum no fingernails.

Foggy the Magnificent (AKA Heathcliffe)

17 hands of idiot horseflesh...
...The one on the left.

What... No Stawberries ripe yet!

guarding the peas

Small pot of jam...

...to small pony

Fierce guard dog

Waiting for spot

Thank you!...

.....for making it this far through my nonsense and meanderings. I hope you have cooked some of the dishes, and enjoyed visiting Britaly. Remember, all you need to get there is love, a full wine cellar and plenty of snacks.

193